THE LIVING COLOR

OF LUKE'S GOSPEL

A DEVOTIONAL

for the age of Jubilee - 2023

David

THE LIVING COLOR
OF LUKE'S GOSPEL

A DEVOTIONAL

by Larry Parsley

A MOCKINGBIRD PUBLICATION
Charlottesville, VA

For Drew, Jack, Timothy, and Laurel,
with joy and deep gratitude

CONTENTS

INTRODUCTION   1

VOILÀ (1:1-2:52)   3
  A Book for God's Friends Everywhere (1:1-4)   5
  When Incense Caught Fire (1:5-17)   7
  Silent Shouts (1:18-25)   9
  The Hidden Audition (1:26-38)   11
  A Delightfully-Overused Word (1:39-45)   13
  Where Do We File This Song? (1:46-56)   15
  Mercy Magnified (1:57-66)   17
  At Last the Sun (1:67-80)   19
  The Miracle in the Mundane (2:1-7)   21
  Shepherdsville (2:8-20)   23
  By the Book (2:21-24)   25
  Arms Finally Full (2:25-35)   27
  Crazy Prayer Lady (2:36-40)   29
  Equally Mystified (2:41-52)   31

STARTLED, NOT CODDLED (3:1-22)   33
  Where the Word Lands (3:1-6)   35
  Too Hot to Handle? (3:7-20)   37
  Costly Words (3:18-20)   39
  The Curtain Parts (3:21-22)   41

THE FIRST 100 DAYS (OR LESS) (3:23-4:44)   43
  Here Comes (Finally) the Son (3:23-38)   45
  The Do-Over (4:1-13)   47
  "When the Sermon Starts Well..." (4:14-22)   49

"...When the Sermon Ends Poorly" (4:23-30)   51

"Be Quiet" (4:31-37)   53

Glimpses Near and Far (4:38-41)   55

Jesus Is Not Running for Mayor (4:42-44)   57

AN ECLECTIC TEAM (5:1-9:50)   59

The Fish Are on the Shore (5:1-11)   61

Can and Will (5:12-13)   63

He Sees All (5:17-26)   65

"Follow Me...to the Exit" (5:27-32)   67

The Fatal Flaw in Competitive
    Religion (5:33-39)   69

Receiving Gifts, Not Abusing Them (6:1-5)   71

Debating the Great Debater (6:6-11)   73

The Jesus Draft (6:12-16)   75

Salve for Stepped-On Toes (6:17-26)   77

Can Jesus Define "Enemy"? (6:27-36)   79

The Benefit of Half-Closed Eyes (6:37-42)   81

When Even Jesus Is Astounded (7:1-10)   83

Stop That Funeral! (7:11-17)   85

Not Quite What We Expected (7:18-23)   87

The Last of His Kind (7:23-35)   89

The Gospel for the Flat Broke (7:36-50)   91

Jesus' Whistlestop Tour (8:1-3)   93

A Documentary on Seeds (8:4-15)   95

Putting His Words Into Play (8:16-21)   97

Have You Not Been
    Paying Attention? (8:22-25)   99

A Gospel for the Other Side (8:26-39)   101

The Signal and the Noise (8:40-56)   103

Unpacking Our Suitcases (9:1-9)   105

Hidden Abundance (9:10-17)   107

True Hope Goes Down with
   the Ship (9:18-27)   109
Try Saying Nothing (9:28-36)   111
A Broken Heart on Display (9:37-42)   113
Adventures in Mis-Translation (9:43-50)   115

ON THE ROAD WITH JESUS (9:51-22:71)   117
Walking an Impossible Line (9:51-56)   119
Jesus' Press Secretary (9:57-62)   121
Planting Peace in a Chaotic World (10:1-24)   123
Go and Do Likewise? (10:25-37)   125
Waiting on Words (10:38-42)   127
A Gift, Not a Chore (11:1-13)   129
Bullying the Bully (11:14-23)   131
Evil in the Attic (11:24-28)   133
Hidden in Plain Sight (11:29-36)   135
The Problem with Surface
   Readings (11:37-54)   137
Learning What to Fear (12:1-12)   139
Praying to Myself (12:13-31)   141
Deconstructing Worry (12:22-34)   143
I'm Awake? (12:35-48)   145
A Different Type of Forecasting (12:49-59)   147
A Momentary Stay of Execuation (13:1-9)   149
Toes to Nose (13:10-21)   151
From Theoretical to Personal (13:22-30)   153
Finishing the Job (13:31-35)   155
A Religion in Need of Healing (14:1-6)   157
Downwardly Mobile (14:7-14)   159
Heartbreak and Hopefulness (14:15-24)   161
The Gospel Is Not a Side Dish (14:25-35)   163
Against My Better Judgment (15:1-10)   165

Theology in Miniature (15:11-32)   167

Blessed Are the Shrewd (16:1-13)   169

Trying to Fool the Scale (16:14-18)   171

Good News Embedded in a
    Nightmare (16:19-31)   173

Attention! (17:1-10)   175

The Real Hero (17:11-19)   177

The Speed of Love (17:20-37)   179

Don't Give Up (18:1-8)   181

"God Have Mercy!" (18:9-14)   183

The Opposite of Social Climbing (18:15-17)   185

The Impossible Possibility (18:18-34)   187

The Shout Above the Shout (18:35-43)   189

An Inexplicable Compulsion (19:1-10)   191

That Blasted Napkin (19:11-27)   193

Enliven Our Stony Hearts (19:28-40)   195

Cleaning House (19:41-48)   197

Auditing Jesus' Credentials (20:1-8)   199

The Thrill of Defeat (20:9-18)   201

When Jesus Blows Our Cover (20:20-26)   203

The Lord of the Living (20:27-40)   205

Seeing Over the Slant (20:41-21:4)   207

Not 'When' or 'What' but 'How' (21:5-28)   209

Reading the Leaves (21:29-38)   211

The Coming Collision (22:1-6)   213

Blessedly Trapped in a Moment (22:7-23)   215

The Greatest (22:24-30)   217

Truth in a Time Capsule (22:31-38)   219

The Bottom of the Staircase (22:39-46)   221

What Adversity Revealed (22:47-53)   223

What the Face Tries to Conceal (22:54-62)   225

Prophet, Priest, and King (22:63-71)   227

"THE LORD HAS
 TAKEN AWAY" (23:1-24:53)   229
When People Show Us Who
 They Are (23:1-7)   231
Jesus, Cornered (23:8-12)   233
Reason v. Rage (23:13-25)   235
The Scene of the Collision (23:26-31)   237
Flipping the Script (23:32-43)   239
When Mockery Melts in
 Our Mouths (23:44-49)   241
Preparing for Opening Day (23:50-56)   243
Gumshoe Angels (24:1-12)   245
The Bread That Makes the
 Sandwich (24:13-27)   247
The Moment of Clarity (24:28-35)   249
The Merry Prankster (24:36-43)   251
You Say Goodbye, but I Say
 Hello (24:44-53)   253

AFTERWORD   255

ENDNOTES   257

Introduction

John McPhee, an award-winning journalist for *The New Yorker*, is as fanatical about structuring his writing as he is researching it. In the Introduction of the first volume of the *John McPhee Reader*, his Princeton colleague William Howarth took journalists inside McPhee's workshop where he produced all those winning *New Yorker* profiles on canoes and pine forests and oranges and so many other subjects rendered intensely interesting by McPhee. After transcribing his interviews, McPhee codes them with key words and writes each key idea on a stack of index cards. "After assembling a stack, he fans them out and begins to play a sort of writer's solitaire, studying the possibilities of order."

When the author of the third gospel was producing his masterwork, he speaks of "eyewitnesses" and traditions "handed down" and items "carefully investigated" in order to produce an "orderly account" (Luke 1:1-3). Such phrases prompt me to imagine Luke's writer's workshop—Luke's "index cards," if you will. His preface modestly informs us that he is not the first author to undertake capturing in print the living color of Jesus' life. He was not an apostolic eyewitness (like tradition ascribes to John or Matthew), nor was he a close associate of the original Twelve (like tradition says Mark was to Peter). What Luke brings, rather, is the historian's gift. He has a system. Yes, Luke will make ready use of the materials already available (what we find, for example, in the earlier gospels of Mark and Matthew), but he will also consult other sources unavailable to us today. And you and I, reader, will be the beneficiaries of Luke's historical research. Luke's account goes beyond the informing function of good journalism, or even the didactic benefit of good theology. Starting with the people who welcomed Jesus into the world, Luke lets Jesus materialize before our eyes as the most intensely interesting subject of any profile ever written.

Throughout this gospel, Luke does all the hard work of presenting Jesus in clarity and beauty. Jesus (as he is remembered by those closest to him), walks, prays, spins stories, heals, confronts, comforts, challenges, suffers, bleeds, dies, rises, and rises some more. The stories flow, one into another, and it is often hard to find a natural stopping point. My modest goal is simply to lay down these hopefully-not-too-annoying speed bumps at regular intervals, helping you to pause long enough to ponder anew the mind-boggling things Jesus says and does and creates and empowers. Along the way, may you play your own kind of faithful solitaire with Luke's sentences and stories, "treasuring up all these things" and "pondering them" in your heart (Luke 2:19).

VOILÀ

(LUKE 1:1-2:52)

The French have a marvelous word, not easily translated in English. Whenever I hear it, I picture some resplendent waiter in a pricey French restaurant, removing the dome from the top of the exquisite dish the chef has prepared, and announcing with no small amount of drama: *voilà*. It is a word we use when some sort of virtuosity is in our midst. In English, we might say, "Look here!" In King James English, we might say, "Behold!"

As Luke opens this gospel, introducing us both to the birth of Jesus and the subsequent birth of his public ministry, "*voilà*" is the persistent tone. In fact, older translations repeatedly use that word "Behold"—especially voiced by angels. Zechariah hears it, and so does Mary.

In these opening chapters, we won't yet meet Jesus, the main course of this gospel. Still, that will not stop us from experiencing that anticipation of what Christ will bring to us. Behold! *Voilà!*

A BOOK FOR GOD'S FRIENDS
EVERYWHERE
(1:1-4)

¹ Many have undertaken to draw up an account of the things that have been fulfilled among us, ² just as they were handed down to us by those who from the first were eyewitnesses and servants of the word. ³ With this in mind, since I myself have carefully investigated everything from the beginning, I too decided to write an orderly account for you, most excellent Theophilus, ⁴ so that you may know the certainty of the things you have been taught.

Like so many modern books, Luke's gospel includes a dedication—to some person addressed as "most excellent Theophilus." *Theophilus* is a Greek word which means "friend of God." Some have conjectured Theophilus to be a wealthy Gentile patron who was keenly interested in Jesus (enough to fund Luke's research). Others have speculated that this term is a stand-in for an anonymous person or even a church.

My goal is not to make a positive identification of the mysterious Theophilus, but rather to ask if we might trace our names over his. I would like to fancy myself as God's friend, even with all my warts and imperfections. I, too, desire to sift through the eyewitness testimony about Jesus. I crave a deeper grounding in the life and work of Jesus. Indeed, what better gift for a "friend of God" than a well-researched account of God's Son?

Jesus, your history is endlessly
fascinating to me.

WHEN INCENSE CAUGHT FIRE
(LUKE 1:5-17)

> *7 But they were childless because Elizabeth was not able to conceive, and they were both very old. 8 Once when Zechariah's division was on duty and he was serving as priest before God, 9 he was chosen by lot, according to the custom of the priesthood, to go into the temple of the Lord and burn incense. 10 And when the time for the burning of incense came, all the assembled worshipers were praying outside. 11 Then an angel of the Lord appeared to him, standing at the right side of the altar of incense. 12 When Zechariah saw him, he was startled and was gripped with fear.*

An old priest, the dutiful husband of a faithful and childless wife, could well have *trudged* into the Temple on that fated day. He had sent so many prayers up to heaven, but so few answers had dropped back down. Still, righteous Zechariah does his duty. During this afternoon prayer service, he is "chosen by lot" (roughly equivalent to the roll of sacred dice) to preside over the holy task of mingling burning coals with dry incense on the altar, as people outside send their own intercessions heavenward.

What Zechariah does not expect (how could he?) is that prayers long past their expiration date will be answered by an angel who travels down the same escalator upon which those prayers arose. It is as if God chooses this time to deliver on so many of those back-ordered prayers—a fruitful womb, a son full of the Holy Spirit, and most importantly a faithful God who is only just beginning to prepare his people for Christ's arrival.

Sometimes, when I am doing the minimal amount of landscaping to stay in good standing with my neighbors, I grow frustrated with what is actually something of a horticultural miracle: green shoots of grass springing up through infinitesimally small cracks in my sidewalk. For Zechariah and Elizabeth, from the flat and lifeless surface of their past, something will soon spring up, bright green with hope.

Jesus, you honor every one of the prayers I fear you have ignored.

SILENT SHOUTS
(LUKE 1:18-25)

18 Zechariah asked the angel, "How can I be sure of this? I am an old man and my wife is well along in years." 19 The angel said to him, "I am Gabriel. I stand in the presence of God, and I have been sent to speak to you and to tell you this good news. 20 And now you will be silent and not able to speak until the day this happens, because you did not believe my words, which will come true at their appointed time."

Old Zechariah asks the question we often ask when faith blows the doors off our worldview: "How?" *How could this good news ever possibly be true?* The angel Gabriel responds to "How" with "Who"—as if to say, "Do you know who I am?" Or better, "Do you truly realize who God is, the one who has dispatched me along with my gift of 'good news'" (v. 19)? In other words, Gabriel does not give an explanation for these glorious mysteries; he simply flashes an ID badge.

What comes next for Zechariah is two "signs," or miracles, the first negative and the second positive. Negatively, Zechariah is struck dumb. Positively, Elizabeth conceives! The first miracle feels punitive to me, and maybe that is its primary purpose. Still, when Zechariah staggers out of the Holy Place after his unexpected audience with Gabriel, some kind of holiness must shimmer off of him, because the waiting people realize he has seen a vision (v. 22). Perhaps there are worse things in life than to enter into an enforced silence as we reflect on God's power and grace. For now, his heart must praise while his lips wait for their opportunity.

In less extraordinary ways, some of the inexplicable punishments of our lives function this way. We stagger as one struck, unable to do what normally comes easily. But in the waiting, God is giving birth to faith in us, and not just faith, but *life*.

Jesus, you speak through the painful and
joyful moments of our days.

THE HIDDEN AUDITION
(LUKE 1:26-38)

[28] The angel went to her and said, "Greetings, you who are highly favored! The Lord is with you." [29] Mary was greatly troubled at his words and wondered what kind of greeting this might be. [30] But the angel said to her, "Do not be afraid, Mary; you have found favor with God. [31] You will conceive and give birth to a son, and you are to call him Jesus.

My junior high drama teacher would affix character names to pieces of construction paper, attach string to them, and loop them over our heads. And so, a shy boy might have "become" *Ebenezer Scrooge* or an exuberant cheerleader *Ophelia*. As fun or as terrifying as those character experiments might have been, when the school bell rang, the placards would be removed, and the boy and girl would resume their typical adolescent roles.

Not so with Mary! Unlike Zechariah and Elizabeth in the previous verses, we know next to nothing about Mary except her hometown of Nazareth, her youthfulness, and her fiancé Joseph. No moral or spiritual qualifications are listed that might prompt the angel Gabriel to begin to lay upon her these outrageously gracious placards: "God's Highly-Favored" and "Mother of

God's Son." God has seemingly held hidden auditions and graciously drafted Mary for this role.

Such grace "greatly troubled" Mary and confused her as well; grace has been doing that for centuries. Ultimately, Mary agrees to play her part. She agrees to be the staging ground for God's gracious words to come true in her (v. 38).

Jesus, you have chosen us, like Mary, to be the theater of your gracious life.

A DELIGHTFULLY OVERUSED
WORD
(LUKE 1:39-45)

*[41] When Elizabeth heard Mary's greeting, the
baby leaped in her womb, and Elizabeth was
filled with the Holy Spirit. [42] In a loud voice
she exclaimed: "Blessed are you among women,
and blessed is the child you will bear!*

What did pre-modern writers do without word proces-
sors? Today, if you are a little worried that you might
have used the word "transform" a few too many times,
you can just right-click the word and replace it with one
of the options the thesaurus function suggests (*alter,
change, evolve*...you get the picture).

Elizabeth, however, seems unbothered by repeti-
tion. When newly-pregnant Mary hurries to greet her
very-pregnant relative Elizabeth, no sooner does she
say hello than John the Fetus begins to do The Wave!
Tiny John, filled with the Holy Spirit *from the womb*
(1:15), "leaped for joy" in awareness that his "Lord"
had drawn near (vv. 43-44). Elizabeth, filled with the
same Spirit, prophesies by over-using the word "bless."
Mary is blessed, her son is blessed, and Elizabeth cannot
believe her good fortune to welcome both of them into
her home. All of this leads Elizabeth to add a closing

benediction, once again to Mary: *"Blessed is she who has believed that the Lord would fulfill his promises to her!"* (v. 45).

I am sure I could never tire of that word. Speak it over me again and again. Tell me repeatedly about the blessing of Jesus, incarnated in Mary, blessing Mary and blessing Elizabeth and her son John, and blessing you too, and anyone *"who has believed that the Lord would fulfill his promises."*

Jesus, you bless us over and over again.

WHERE DO WE FILE THIS SONG?
(LUKE 1:46-56)

[46] And Mary said: "My soul glorifies the Lord [47] and my spirit rejoices in God my Savior, [48] for he has been mindful of the humble state of his servant. From now on all generations will call me blessed, [49] for the Mighty One has done great things for me—holy is his name.

Mary's song (often called by its Latin name, the "Magnificat") positions Mary as a kind of crossover artist. As the song opens—"My soul magnifies the Lord"—I can almost picture Mary as Fraulein Maria in *The Sound of Music*, twirling and belting out her wonder over God's goodness. But if the song starts off feeling like a **showtune**, it transitions in the middle stanzas to something more like a 1960s **protest song**. Depending on where you sit in the social order of things, the song either delights (God has "exalted those of humble estate") or disturbs ("the rich he has sent away empty"). Before the song wraps up, Mary sneaks in a **folk ballad** to Abraham, her ancestor, who first heard God whisper the outrageous promises that are now coming true in her womb.

It may be that you need this medley to minister to you in a variety of ways today. You may need a strong dose of Mary's wonder at God's creative artistry brushed upon the humblest of canvases. Or you may need to feel God's law protesting your attachment to the world's toys and your pretty sorry job of sharing them with your neighbor.

Still, however low this song might drop you, remember that what God promised Abraham and Mary, in Christ God also promises you: "his mercy is for those who fear him from generation to generation" (v. 50). If I'm doing the math right, that includes your generation as well.

Jesus, your mercy is its own kind of music.

MERCY MAGNIFIED
(LUKE 1:57-66)

⁶³ [Zechariah] asked for a writing tablet, and to everyone's astonishment he wrote, "His name is John." ⁶⁴ Immediately his mouth was opened and his tongue set free, and he began to speak, praising God. ⁶⁵ All the neighbors were filled with awe, and throughout the hill country of Judea people were talking about all these things. ⁶⁶ Everyone who heard this wondered about it, asking, "What then is this child going to be?" For the Lord's hand was with him.

My wife and I are blessed with four children, and I cried every time a new one came into this world. If you ask me, every birth is miraculous and a cause for raucous celebration. Still, no offense to any of my four kids, John's birth was bigger. It triggered a flood of mercy that poured over the levies of his village.

Why do I say this? As we've already seen, after so many years of suffering, an old "barren" woman has given birth. Luke claims this miracle is in fact a sign that God has (literally) "magnified" his mercy in Elizabeth just like with Mary, and this great mercy has provided an occasion for joyful celebration (v. 58). That miracle could have merely entered the lore of Zechariah and Elizabeth's family tree, but God's mercy continued to show itself in the process of naming the baby. Not content with calling him "Little Zechariah,"[1] as the neighbors naturally assumed, his mother boldly speaks up and says to call him "John" (a name which means "Yahweh has shown favor"), a name embedded with God's mercy. I'm guessing the guests at the circumcision ceremony assumed poor old Elizabeth was exhausted, post-pregnancy, and so they take the extraordinary step of appealing to her incapacitated husband, struck dumb many months back. But when he calls for a legal pad and pen and scrawls out J-O-H-N, mercy frees his vocal chords, and the language he shouts is Praise (v. 64).

The guests commenced to gossip this merciful news all through the hill country, and a sense of faithful expectancy was palpable: "What then is this child going to be?" Indeed.

Jesus, your mercy never stops flowing.

AT LAST THE SUN
(LUKE 1:67-80)

67 His father Zechariah was filled with the Holy Spirit and prophesied: 68 "Praise be to the Lord, the God of Israel, because he has come to his people and redeemed them. 69 He has raised up a horn of salvation for us in the house of his servant David 70 (as he said through his holy prophets of long ago) …

In my mid-20s, my pastoral responsibilities included serving as a minister to senior adults. It was comical, really: this kid fresh out of seminary, "leading" World War II veterans. Still, I thrilled at the opportunity to feel like I was shaking hands with history, including a man named Otto, then in his 90s, a soldier in World War I.

When the formerly faithless Zechariah is filled with the Holy Spirit, he offers up this prophetic song called the "Benedictus" (widely sung today). And in doing so, Zechariah shows a familiarity with a history that extends long before his birth. It is as if the Spirit grants Zechariah a vision that extends back to Israel's birth, back to Father Abraham (v. 73). Zechariah sings praises to the God who once "visited" his people in the Exodus and is now preparing to visit again. The God who comes down to visit also raises up a "horn of salvation."

(Whenever you see that word "horn," reflect upon the strength of some powerful animal.)

I could not imagine all the pain that Otto's eyes had witnessed, but I treasured the chance to sit in his presence. Old Zechariah, filling in for Old Israel, has so many memories of dark days and the hatred from enemies (v. 71) that this son he holds in his arms brings him so much joy. John's birth is a signal that "the rising sun will come to us from heaven" (v. 78). Zechariah is cradling holy history in his arms.

Jesus, you visit the troubled with
a promise of hope.

THE MIRACLE IN
THE MUNDANE
(LUKE 2:1-7)

> *⁶ While they were there, the time came for the baby to be born, ⁷ and she gave birth to her firstborn, a son. She wrapped him in cloths and placed him in a manger, because there was no guest room available for them."*

In this passage, there are two sections which begin with a Greek phrase that means "it happened." There are two big "happenings," in other words. The first happening is that the guy who thinks he rules the world, Caesar Augustus, decrees a census as a precursor to taxation (you have to know where your people live before you can break their piggy banks). Caesar's decree, the first domino, eventually triggers a reaction that propels Joseph of Nazareth toward his ancestral home in Bethlehem.

The second "happening" (v. 6) speaks to a deeper decree. Mary, fiancée of Joseph, gives birth to a son, whom we will come to understand as not just her "firstborn" (v. 7) but the "firstborn over all creation" (Colossians 1:15).

In one sense, what happens in this short passage is so predictable: laws are issued, taxes are levied, babies are born. These kinds of things happen every day. And yet, this common scene has become one of the most performed children's plays in history. Perhaps you've witnessed it or even starred in it: a young boy and young girl, in bathrobes, he with a staff and she with a doll, trying not to walk too fast up the church aisle and toward the manger on the stage. The first decree is mundane—taxes are always being issued. But that second decree? God, the one who is really in charge, authorizing the birth of his only Son into human extremity? That is the miracle in the mundane.

*Jesus, help us find something miraculous in
the mundane moments of this day.*

SHEPHERDSVILLE
(LUKE 2:8-20)

13 Suddenly a great company of the heavenly host appeared with the angel, praising God and saying 14 "Glory to God in the highest heaven, and on earth peace to those on whom his favor rests." 15 When the angels had left them and gone into heaven, the shepherds said to one another, "Let's go to Bethlehem and see this thing that has happened, which the Lord has told us about."

I hear these feel-good stories all the time. A famous musician swings into town for a concert. On the local news the next day, you learn how the musician gave premium tickets and backstage passes to disadvantaged youth who could not have afforded to even buy popcorn for the event.

The shepherds in today's passage are at the center of such a story. God, who loves all people, *all* people, seems to have a special place in his heart for shepherds. Bethlehem is the hometown of King David, a local-shepherd-made-good. Psalm 23 says that God himself is a shepherd, and Jesus in John 10 self-identifies as the Good Shepherd. Israel had experienced her fill of false shepherds, the kind who eat the sheep (Ezekiel 34). But now, in Shepherdsville a different kind of shepherd will be born, appropriately enough, among domestic animals and a cattle trough. The basic message the angels communicate to Bethlehem's shepherds is: "God has chosen you to be among the first to see it. Here are your backstage passes."

Like excited teenagers, witnessing a heavenly concert for free, these bleary-eyed shepherds race backstage to see the child up close. And on their way back, they could not stop praising God. Can you blame them?

Jesus, you embody a shepherd's heart for us all.

BY THE BOOK
(LUKE 2:21-24)

²¹ On the eighth day, when it was time to circumcise the child, he was named Jesus, the name the angel had given him before he was conceived. ²² When the time came for the purification rites required by the Law of Moses, Joseph and Mary took him to Jerusalem to present him to the Lord ²³ (as it is written in the Law of the Lord, "Every firstborn male is to be consecrated to the Lord"), ²⁴ and to offer a sacrifice in keeping with what is said in the Law of the Lord: "a pair of doves or two young pigeons."

One of the frequent criticisms leveled at Jesus is that he is a Lawbreaker. He and his disciples hang out with people who live on the wrong side of the Law, and he and his disciples could stand to be a little more rigorous about washing their hands and following the myriad of restrictions which had sprouted up around the Sabbath.

How ironic are these complaints, since Jesus memorably says that he did not come to "abolish" God's laws but rather to "fulfill them" (Matthew 5:17). The above passage demonstrates that even baby Jesus was a Law-Keeper (or at least his parents were). On the correct day (the eighth), Jesus received the correct covenant sign (circumcision), to be followed by the correct sacrifices offered to purify his mother. Jesus' parents, too poor to offer the normally expected sacrifice of a lamb, nevertheless made the offering of birds—signifying that this child was the firstborn, and the firstborn belonged to God (Numbers 18:15).

Think about it: this child will fulfill the Law until the very end. This child, God's one and only Son, will become the Lamb the world is much too poor to afford.

Jesus, we behold you as the Lamb of God.

ARMS FINALLY FULL
(LUKE 2:25-35)

> [27] ...*When the parents brought in the child Jesus...,* [28] *Simeon took him in his arms and praised God, saying:* [29] *"Sovereign Lord, as you have promised, you may now dismiss your servant in peace.* [30] *For my eyes have seen your salvation,* [31] *which you have prepared in the sight of all nations:* [32] *a light for revelation to the Gentiles, and the glory of your people Israel."*

Somewhere, on a VHS tape in the bottom of a cardboard box, there is footage of one of my infant sons being dedicated at church. I started out holding him, swaying side to side as I tried to keep him calm, and then my wife took him. The video shows me, arms now empty, still rocking back and forth (looking goofy, I must admit). Still, once you've held a child you've long awaited, it does something permanent to your sense of rhythm.

Simeon might back me up on this. For years, he awoke with a hope that this might be the day that he would hold, not *his* infant, per se, but the *world's* child. And one day, the Holy Spirit whispered to Simeon, "It's time." Simeon presides over a worship service like no other. Taking the child in his arms, Simeon tells God,

"I can die now!" (which is something you don't often hear in church). He praises God that this infant will become a beacon to draw in outsiders (Gentiles) and cause rejoicing for insiders (Israel).

Unfortunately, Simeon intimates, this glory won't come without a cost. The mother of the Suffering Servant will not come out unscathed (v. 35). Sorrow will precede healing. As commentator G.B. Caird has put it, many (like Peter, like Paul, like us) will have to fail and fall before we rise in grace.

Jesus, in your rising, we rise.

CRAZY PRAYER LADY
(LUKE 2:36-40)

[36] There was also a prophet, Anna, the daughter of Penuel, of the tribe of Asher. She was very old; she had lived with her husband seven years after her marriage, [37] and then was a widow until she was eighty-four. She never left the temple but worshiped night and day, fasting and praying. [38] Coming up to them at that very moment, she gave thanks to God and spoke about the child to all who were looking forward to the redemption of Jerusalem.

At a pastors' lunch a friend, with a hint of a grin, asked the rest of us: "Do you guys have a 'crazy prayer lady' at your church?" I knew instantly what he meant. Many churches I have attended had people who were unusually devoted to prayer, and sometimes they have struggled with their slacker pastors over how to stoke the furnace of prayer at church.

Anna is a Crazy Prayer Lady (in the best sense of that awkward phrase). Hers is a story of long-lasting pain, having been a widow longer than most have been alive. Yet, like her namesake Hannah (1 Samuel 1-2), Anna has forged her pain into prayer. Day and night, likely thin as a rail from her fasting, she prophesies to bystanders and cries out for God to grant barren Israel a child.

Now, like an eager family that arrives at the parade hours before it begins, Anna has the best view of the long-awaited child in Simeon's arms. Now, all prophecy turns to praise. She has seen with her own eyes what the world would soon see in Jesus—"the grace of God was on him" (v. 40).

Jesus, you evoke our extroverted praise.

EQUALLY MYSTIFIED
(LUKE 2:41-52)

> *[46] After three days they found him in the temple courts, sitting among the teachers, listening to them and asking them questions. [47] Everyone who heard him was amazed at his understanding and his answers. [48] When his parents saw him, they were astonished. His mother said to him, "Son, why have you treated us like this? Your father and I have been anxiously searching for you." [49] "Why were you searching for me?" he asked. "Didn't you know I had to be in my Father's house?"*

Chances are, no matter how old you are, you've felt that familiar terror. Perhaps you were a child in a grocery store, and you lingered away from the produce aisle and toward the toy aisle, only to look up and find your parent was gone. Maybe you were a parent, and in the mere seconds it took you to select a truly ripe cantaloupe, your precious child was nowhere in sight. Whether you were the child or the parent, in that moment, your mind went to a dark place.

For Mary and Joseph, however, their parental terror plays out, not for moments, but for *three days*. Every year, you see, the Nazareth contingent traveled in packs to the Passover, parents in one throng, kids in another, and everyone was always safely accounted for, eventually. But when his parents decided to check in with 12-year-old Jesus on the return trip, his absence led them on a mad scramble back to Jerusalem. When they finally found him (confounding learned rabbis with his questions and answers), they confronted their son.

What strikes me is that both the parents and their son were equally mystified by one another. Mary could not imagine why her son would treat his parents so disrespectfully. Jesus, in turn, was not flirting with disobedience (v. 51) but practicing a higher allegiance to his Heavenly Father. For Jesus, the greatest terror is not drifting from his earthly parents but straying too far from his "Father's house" (v. 49) and his Father's mission to rescue us.

Jesus, your extreme devotion to your Father is for our eternal benefit.

STARTLED, NOT CODDLED

(LUKE 3:1-22)

Sometimes I wonder what to do with John the Baptist. He is the classic outsider. He prefers shouting to speaking and manages to avoid any urge to speak diplomatically about the failings of his fellow citizens. Candidly, I am not sure I would hire him for any church role that requires a soft touch with seasoned members.

Of course, God did not consult me when calling John the Baptist to prepare the way for Jesus. In the "fullness of time" (Galatians 4:4 ESV), first-century Israel needed to be startled, not coddled. They needed someone with the ego strength to confront just about anyone within earshot, yet with the humility to walk off the stage right when his popularity began to soar. Israel needed John the Baptist, and so do we.

WHERE THE WORD LANDS
(LUKE 3:1-6)

> *¹ In the fifteenth year of the reign of Tiberius Caesar—when Pontius Pilate was governor of Judea, Herod tetrarch of Galilee, his brother Philip tetrarch of Iturea and Traconitis, and Lysanias tetrarch of Abilene— ² during the high-priesthood of Annas and Caiaphas, the word of God came to John son of Zechariah in the wilderness.*

One of the most dramatic moments in even the most boring wedding receptions occurs when the bride turns her back to her closest friends, grips her bouquet, and tosses it blindly over her head. While onlookers may bet on the tallest or most nimble or most assertive of her friends, no one really knows in whose hands the bouquet will land.

Reading the opening words of Chapter 3, I get the funny image of God's Word sailing over the heads of those whom Israel would have recognized as authoritative. It flies over the most well-known man on earth, the Roman Emperor Tiberius, as well as all his governors and rulers in that region. And if that's not surprising, God's Word also bypasses the most powerful religious leaders in the land—the high priests Annas and Caiaphas.

The Word finally lands upon John the Baptist, one of two miracle babies introduced to us in the opening chapters of this gospel. From one vantage point, John resembles an ancient drifter, camping out in the wilderness, far from the halls of political and religious power. In Luke 3, however, this loner finds himself the center of attraction as God's Word energizes his electric preaching and baptizing. John's sermons are harsh and uncompromising, but his promises (then and now) are sweet. As Isaiah dreamed, John would remove obstacles, and repair roads, and prepare the way for Jesus' unhindered access to us. So that, in Christ, "all people will see God's salvation."

Jesus, clear any obstacles that hinder
our view of you.

TOO HOT TO HANDLE?
(LUKE 3:7-20)

15 The people were waiting expectantly and were all wondering in their hearts if John might possibly be the Messiah. 16 John answered them all, "I baptize you with water. But one who is more powerful than I will come, the straps of whose sandals I am not worthy to untie. He will baptize you with the Holy Spirit and fire. 17 His winnowing fork is in his hand to clear his threshing floor and to gather the wheat into his barn, but he will burn up the chaff with unquenchable fire."

In this current era of rapidly declining church attendance, I cannot even comprehend John's church growth strategy. I mean, his revival is working! All kinds of crowds are rushing toward him, including devout Jews and sketchy tax collectors and hardened soldiers. They all left busy lives to travel long distances for the "John-the-Baptist experience," taking notes on his sermons and submitting to his baptism. And instead of handing these guests a cup of coffee and a new member packet, John appears furious that they came at all.

He not only preaches that the ax is at the root of spiritually fruitless trees (v. 9), he practically delights in swinging a rhetorical ax himself. He is completely unimpressed by what is typically impressive—that these sons and daughters of the revolution can trace their lineage back to Abraham. Instead, he demands repentance, generosity, simplicity, and gentleness from the very constituencies that seek him out.

Sometimes, we can mistake the fire-breathers for the Fire, but John won't let us. He lays down God's uncompromising Law so that all who hear will cry out for the only One who can truly baptize us "with the Holy Spirit and fire" (v. 16).

Jesus, help us distinguish you from John, and purify us with your incendiary presence.

COSTLY WORDS
(LUKE 3:18-20)

*18 And with many other words John exhort-
ed the people and proclaimed the good news
to them. 19 But when John rebuked Herod the
tetrarch because of his marriage to Herodias,
his brother's wife, and all the other evil things
he had done, 20 Herod added this to them all:
He locked John up in prison.*

In these early chapters, Luke has swung the spotlight
back and forth, first toward John and then toward Jesus.
We see the common elements of their holy stories—
their surprised parents, their unexpected births, and
their young seriousness about God. In this passage,
however, the baton is being passed from John to Jesus.

Still, I am not prepared for the abrupt transition
between v. 18 and v. 19. In v. 18, John's "many" words
bring the "good news" to his hearers. In v. 19, however,
one of the recipients of John's words reacts negatively
to them. John has specifically called out Herod and his
sister-in-law Herodias, with whom Herod is having an
affair. While we will briefly see John once more in this
gospel (Chapter 7), here it feels like his official ministry
is done. John's words could have brought both Herod
and Herodias to repentance; instead, these two fall
deeper into evil by trying to silence John's message.

Ultimately Jesus will surpass John with his "many" words of good news, as well as words that pierce his hearers to the heart. Jesus' gospel words will likewise sign his death warrant—they are words underwritten by blood.

Jesus, you love us enough to speak
the costly truth.

THE CURTAIN PARTS
(LUKE 3:21-22)

²¹ When all the people were being baptized, Jesus was baptized too. And as he was praying, heaven was opened ²² and the Holy Spirit descended on him in bodily form like a dove. And a voice came from heaven: "You are my Son, whom I love; with you I am well pleased."

In my elementary school cafeteria, we rarely noticed the red curtain. We were busy eating our lunches, telling jokes, and swapping desserts. But a few times a year, that red curtain would open, and our eyes would be transfixed upon the high schoolers who sang and danced and entertained us from the stage.

It is not easy to tell from today's passage how many of those being baptized understood that a curtain was drawing open. But Jesus does. As he emerges from the waters of baptism in prayer, we readers of this gospel are treated to a powerful play where each member of the Trinity plays a role. As Jesus prays, Heaven's curtains part and Jesus feels the Spirit rest upon him "in bodily form like a dove" (v. 22). Now, the Father can no longer contain his pride and joy. *This, world, is my beloved son, and you could never comprehend the joy and delight he brings me.*

In Jesus, we rise as the curtain that separates heaven and earth parts. In Jesus, his Spirit also rests upon us. In Jesus, we discover how God feels about those blessed enough to find themselves *in Christ*—*"well-pleased"*!

Jesus, you share your Spirit and God's joy
with us.

THE FIRST 100 DAYS
(OR LESS)

(LUKE 3:23-4:44)

Type in "first 100 days" into a bookstore search bar and you will find histories of presidential administrations and advice for CEOs, salespeople, nurses, Human Resources specialists, and pastors. One thing is clear: there is a strong consensus that our opening acts can determine the success of the whole play.

When thirty-year-old Jesus steps onto the stage, his extraordinary deeds and words signal that we have never seen a leader like this. His first forty days are spent *out of view*, in the wilderness, with nothing but the Holy Spirit to sustain him in his combat with evil. And when he returns, this same Spirit breathes through Jesus' powerful preaching and healing. It won't take a hundred days to know this is like nothing we've ever seen before.

HERE COMES (FINALLY)
THE SON
(LUKE 3:23-38)

*23 Now Jesus himself was about thirty years old
when he began his ministry. He was the son, so
it was thought, of Joseph, the son of Heli, 24 the
son of Matthat, the son of Levi…*

I will not ask you if you read every word of today's passage (if you did, congratulations!). I won't try to see if
you can distinguish the Mattathias of v. 25 from the
Mattathias of v. 26 (I cannot). I will not spend time
speculating about reasons for the differences between
Matthew's genealogy (which starts with Abraham and
moves forward to Jesus) and Luke's (which starts with
Jesus and his stepfather Joseph and moves backward,
beyond Abraham to "Adam, the son of God" (v. 38).

I will simply ask you to consider that this thirty-
year-old Jesus who launches his ministry is not only
God's son (v. 22) but also a direct descendant of the
human race, with all its promise and folly. Jesus came
from these people, and Jesus came *for* these people and
their people's people. This procession of these names
sing their own strange hymn of praise to God's Son and
Earth's native son.

One night last December, I stood out in the mist
at a local cemetery, listening as a speaker solemnly

pronounced the names of children and teenagers from our community who had died through the years. A name was read, family and friends stepped forward, and flowers were gently placed upon a giant, makeshift altar. To the uninitiated, it may have seemed like an endless recitation. But not to those who loved these sons and daughters, nor to the Savior who came to reclaim all the forgotten descendants of Adam.

Jesus, you came to call each of us by name.

THE DO-OVER
(LUKE 4:1-13)

> [1] *Jesus, full of the Holy Spirit, left the Jordan and was led by the Spirit into the wilderness,* [2] *where for forty days he was tempted by the devil. He ate nothing during those days, and at the end of them he was hungry.*

"We want a do-over!" This was the frequent cry on our baseball sandlot growing up. Maybe the batter wasn't ready when the pitch was thrown. Or the base (a frisbee or spare baseball glove) slipped out from under the runner when he slid. Whatever the reason, the petitioner wanted another chance to be successful.

When the Spirit leads Jesus into the wilderness to conduct a forty-day spiritual battle with the devil, Jesus facilitates a do-over that Israel neither deserved nor even requested. Israel had wandered in the wilderness for forty *years*, and when tempted, Israel performed badly. As the Psalmists frequently recount (see Psalm 106),[2] Israel failed by craving bread and bowing down to a golden calf and repeatedly testing God's patience. Some Israelites even preferred the sovereignty of Pharaoh, who had enslaved them, over the God who was leading them to freedom.

Enter Jesus. He parries the thrusts of Satan at every turn, hungering for a deeper bread, refusing to bend the knee to earthbound power, and defying Satan's invitation to test God by launching himself from Jerusalem's temple. In Jesus, we get our do-over—indeed, endless do-overs—He will secure our victory, even if it means he must one day refuse to jump down from Jerusalem's cross.

Jesus, in your grace I am finally victorious.

"WHEN THE SERMON
STARTS WELL…"
(LUKE 4:14-22)

17 and the scroll of the prophet Isaiah was handed to him. Unrolling it, he found the place where it is written: 18 "The Spirit of the Lord is on me, because he has anointed me to proclaim good news to the poor. He has sent me to proclaim freedom for the prisoners and recovery of sight for the blind, to set the oppressed free, 19 to proclaim the year of the Lord's favor."

It is hard to imagine a better launch to Jesus' public ministry. The Holy Spirit accompanies him; his face is above the fold in all Galilean newspapers; people can't stop talking about his sermons; and "everyone praised him" (v. 15). And can you conceive a more stunning launch to a sermon than the one presented to the hometown crowd in Nazareth?

When Jesus received the Isaiah scroll that Sabbath day, he knew the precise spot he was looking for. Jesus reads those familiar words from Isaiah 61 about God's servant, soaked in the Spirit, who will one day walk through Israel's streets tossing out good news like candy from a parade float. The poor and captive, the blind and oppressed? Every one will walk home with grace falling out of their stuffed pockets.

Jesus reads holy words about what must surely feel like a futuristic dream, as the organ softly plays "in the sweet, by and by…" He sits down to teach, as was the custom, and says, in essence, "The future is now." Turn the calendar, because the "year of the Lord's favor" starts today (v. 19).

Jesus, the "year" of your favor never ends.

"...WHEN THE SERMON ENDS POORLY" (LUKE 4:23-30)

²³ Jesus said to them, "Surely you will quote this proverb to me: 'Physician, heal yourself!' And you will tell me, 'Do here in your hometown what we have heard that you did in Capernaum.'" ²⁴ "Truly I tell you," he continued, "no prophet is accepted in his hometown."

The preacher in me wonders if Jesus should have stopped while he was ahead. After all, when he first began this sermon, "all spoke well" of his "gracious words" (v. 22). Jesus, however, knew his grace could not yet find root in the prideful hearts of his fellow citizens. He speaks as a prophet, after all, and not as his hometown's public relations officer.

Nazareth thinks that, if any town should be the beneficiary of Jesus' free healthcare, it should be them. Yet Jesus knows that their collective pride and unbelief will prevent the medicine of his gospel from addressing their deepest wounds. Instead, like Elijah and Elisha before him, Jesus will do his best work outside places of religious self-importance. Gentiles and foreigners will actually experience the signs and wonders Nazareth demands. Nazareth wants their native son to flatter them, but Jesus, God's son, has a deeper obligation—to speak prophetic truth to his hometown (v. 24).

No matter how much we hate when Jesus preaches the Law, our actions prove his point with gloomy consistency. Tragically, some would rather kill the Great Physician (v. 29) than accept his devastating diagnosis.

Jesus, forgive us for bristling at your
painful words.

"BE QUIET"
(LUKE 4:31-37)

33 In the synagogue there was a man possessed by a demon, an impure spirit. He cried out at the top of his voice, 34 "Go away! What do you want with us, Jesus of Nazareth? Have you come to destroy us? I know who you are —the Holy One of God!" 35 "Be quiet!" Jesus said sternly. "Come out of him!" Then the demon threw the man down before them all and came out without injuring him. 36 All the people were amazed and said to each other, "What words these are! With authority and power he gives orders to impure spirits and they come out!"

Do you have one of these people in your life? That annoying sibling or acquaintance who shouts out random digits when you're trying to remember a phone number? Or that person who, candidly, will not *shut up* when you are trying to think?

I don't mean to trivialize demonic oppression (by any means!), but I do think of that loud person when I read this passage. One Sabbath day, Jesus enters Capernaum's synagogue, where the residents of that fishing village sit in awed attention, inhaling his dazzling and authoritative words. That's when a demon, using his human victim as a ventriloquist's dummy, desperately distracts the crowd with crazed shouts. The demon is at once combative and terrified.

Jesus "sternly" addresses the demon: "Be quiet!" (v. 35), and the demon flees. Now, in the awed silence, the listeners have the opportunity to internalize Jesus' powerful words. Likely whispering, they say to one another: "What words these are!" (v. 36).

Dear reader, I hope you experience at least one moment of authentic peace and quiet today. I pray that Jesus Himself speaks "sternly" to your screaming thoughts and louder fears. In the grace of that stillness, no matter how long it lasts, may you have space to reflect on Jesus' authoritative words and deeds.

"Consequently, faith comes from hearing the message, and the message is heard through the word about Christ." (Romans 10:17)

GLIMPSES NEAR AND FAR
(LUKE 4:38-41)

[39] So he bent over her and rebuked the fever, and it left her. She got up at once and began to wait on them. [40] At sunset, the people brought to Jesus all who had various kinds of sickness, and laying his hands on each one, he healed them.

A Facebook friend shared photos of his son's graduation from a military academy. These professionally done photos combined vivid closeups of exuberant young men and women tossing hats into the air with an aerial backdrop of jets flying over the stadium. Skillfully that photographer captured the grandeur of the event; Luke does something similar in today's passage. Like a photojournalist, he shares the small exuberances and grand panorama of what happens when Jesus comes to your town.

We begin with the closeups (vv. 38-39). One man (Simon) escorts Jesus to his home near Capernaum's synagogue. In the first image, Jesus stands over the bed of Simon's mother-in-law as she is held in the clutches of a high fever. In the second image, she stands, liberated from her sickness, and serves the seated Jesus at the table.

Next, Luke shoots some landscape photos. We see one shot of the sun setting on a Sabbath day, and villagers (now free from Sabbath restrictions) rushing to Simon's back porch, carrying their sick with them. From an aerial perspective, Jesus looks like a president in an inauguration parade, reaching out his healing hands in all directions.

In the gallery of your mind, can you see it? Can you watch the desperate pleas for help? Can you marvel at Jesus' acts of liberation and healing and watch the expressions of wonder and joy? This is a photoshoot of the gospel.

Jesus, "bend over us" today (v. 39).

JESUS IS NOT RUNNING
FOR MAYOR
(LUKE 4:42-44)

⁴² At daybreak, Jesus went out to a solitary place. The people were looking for him and when they came to where he was, they tried to keep him from leaving them. ⁴³ But he said, "I must proclaim the good news of the kingdom of God to the other towns also, because that is why I was sent." ⁴⁴ And he kept on preaching in the synagogues of Judea.

A few chapters from now (Luke 8), we will learn that when Jesus heals someone, he feels "power go out" from him. Consider, then, how *drained* Jesus must have felt on this Sunday morning, after an entire Sabbath day filled with teaching, healings, and exorcisms.

Luke tells us that when day breaks, Jesus leaves the city of Capernaum (densely peopled with His newfound fans) and searches for a "solitary" place (v. 42). Mark tells us that Jesus did this in order to pray. Jesus' solitude, however, is short-lived. Townspeople track him, find him, and try "to keep him from leaving them." There is a fine line, but a clear line, that stands between our desire to abide with Jesus and our wish to co-opt Jesus. The illustration is imperfect, but a mother's heart warms to the four-year-old who sleeps in her arms but struggles when she refuses to let her get up and fix dinner.

Jesus' response strikes me as both loving yet firm. He has a calling to share with other towns the good news of the Kingdom which Capernaum has witnessed. His role is bigger than just being Mayor of the Village of Me. His grace is as much for my neighbor as for me.

Jesus, your reign exceeds
my little part of the world.

AN ECLECTIC TEAM

(LUKE 5:1-9:50)

Among the many mysterious things we will see in the next five chapters of Luke are the odd people Jesus selects for His team and the odd ways he recruits and empowers them.

In Chapter 5, Jesus begins to reel in Simon Peter on a fishing trip, and he invites Levi to walk off the job —a lucrative gig at the tax office. He stays up all night praying before he makes an official offer to his twelve closest disciples, and one of those offer letters is given to a future "traitor" (6:12-16). Later, we discover that Rabbi Jesus has welcomed women into the ranks of his disciples (8:1-3).

Jesus coaches this team not from a remove but by sharing his power and his mission with them (9:1-2). While Jesus' teammates will continually misunderstand him and even disappoint him, he perseveres with them until the end. Jesus has chosen his own eclectic means to change the world.

THE FISH ARE ON
THE SHORE
(LUKE 5:1-11)

> *⁴ When he had finished speaking, he said to Simon, "Put out into deep water, and let down the nets for a catch." ⁵ Simon answered, "Master, we've worked hard all night and haven't caught anything. But because you say so, I will let down the nets." ⁶ When they had done so, they caught such a large number of fish that their nets began to break.*

Have you ever met folks who, because they are so clearly successful in their own professions, fancy themselves experts in *your* line of work? I have. "Pastor, I think your sermons are getting a little...well...predictable. I'd try maybe finding a new source of illustrations, perhaps?" *Sure*, I think, *I've spent three years in seminary and ten years doing this gig, but of course, you're the expert!*

Is that the kind of passive-aggressive thinking going through Peter's mind when Jesus, after commandeering Peter's boat as a makeshift pulpit, seems to begin giving Peter fishing advice? To his credit, Peter takes Jesus at his word ("because you say so"—v. 5). At Jesus' instruction, these tired, experienced fishermen (who have already trolled this lake during the prime catching time of the evening), wearily truck their nets back in the boats and row out to the magical spot where Jesus is pointing.

What happens next can only be described as holy chaos. Nets overflow with fish and then tear, another boat is summoned, both boats fill with fish, and both boats begin to sink. Peter's chaotic heart also sinks with guilt in the presence of One who has such holy insight (v. 8). Jesus chooses this moment to sink the hook. On Peter's greatest and never-to-be-repeated day as professional fisherman, he is invited by Jesus to redirect his nets toward all those spiritually starving people swarming like fish on the nearby shore. *From now on*, Jesus says, *fish for them.*

> *Jesus, you continue to dazzle*
> *unworthy sinners like us.*

CAN AND WILL
(LUKE 5:12-13)

¹² While Jesus was in one of the towns, a man came along who was covered with leprosy. When he saw Jesus, he fell with his face to the ground and begged him, "Lord, if you are willing, you can make me clean." ¹³ Jesus reached out his hand and touched the man. "I am willing," he said. "Be clean!" And immediately the leprosy left him.

What a loaded request this leper makes to Jesus! The words trigger a certain queasiness in me about the efficacy of prayer: *"Lord, if you are willing, you can make me clean."*

Our doubts about prayer often revolve around those twins, "if" and "can." The first word, "if," questions Jesus' love for us, or at least how we might interpret what a loving Lord might do to help us in our affliction. Our temptation here is to doubt Christ's *mercy.* We envision a God who is indifferent to our suffering, unwilling to help us. That second word, "can," exposes another level of doubt, this time about Christ's *power.* We wonder, in our weakest moments, if Christ's palms are lifted upward at shoulder-height in a kind of shrug: "I wish I could help you, I really do. But your problems are more complicated than my limited powers can handle."

If you catalog the many requests you have made for divine healing in the past, requests not answered in the way you desired, this account may trigger confusion and pain. I am not competent to cipher out the specifics of Christ's interactions with human sickness. But I still take comfort in this confident answer about Christ's heart toward the hurting: *"I am willing,"* he said. *"Be clean!"* This is mercy and power, in equal and lavish portions, extended immediately toward the leper. From now on, the formerly outcast leper will rejoin society, while the newly famous Jesus finds himself fleeing to society's margins. Such mercy and power do not come without a price.

Jesus, your mercy and power are
inextricably linked.

HE SEES ALL
(LUKE 5:17-26)

22 Jesus knew what they were thinking and asked, "Why are you thinking these things in your hearts? 23 Which is easier: to say, 'Your sins are forgiven,' or to say, 'Get up and walk'? 24 But I want you to know that the Son of Man has authority on earth to forgive sins." So he said to the paralyzed man, "I tell you, get up, take your mat and go home." 25 Immediately he stood up in front of them, took what he had been lying on and went home praising God.

If you had been there that day, you would have witnessed some remarkable scenes. For one, you could not have missed the group of religious dignitaries, sitting like exalted tennis judges, eager to catch Jesus in a fault. Your attention would have then been distracted by four friends carrying a fifth man, and the fifth a paralytic. Your eyes would've been glued to this delegation as they attempted first to enter the packed house where Jesus was teaching, and then improvise an aerial drop through the roof! You would have observed the argument that ensued with the religious leaders when Jesus pronounced forgiveness on the paralytic, and the impromptu celebration that was sparked when the same man *walked home!* In other words, you would have seen enough to enthrall you for the rest of your earthly days.

But whatever you might have seen that day, realize that Jesus saw more. Jesus somehow saw both the sins of the paralytic and the "faith" of the paralytic's friends. He saw the proud thoughts of his religious critics, and he foresaw the price to be paid for confounding them with his miraculous healing power.

Even now, Jesus sees our proud thoughts, our fear, our sin, and whatever vestiges there are of our faith. He sees all, and still pronounces a forgiveness and freedom we don't deserve. Our response should mirror the crowd's: *"We have seen remarkable things today."*

Jesus, your love is not limited by what you see.

"FOLLOW ME...TO THE EXIT"
(LUKE 5:27-32)

²⁷ After this, Jesus went out and saw a tax col-
lector by the name of Levi sitting at his tax
booth. "Follow me," Jesus said to him, ²⁸ and
Levi got up, left everything and followed him.

It is only natural that you and I read the Bible like a
screenplay we film in our own heads, supplying our own
casting and set design and improvisation of lines. For
most of my life, I've read today's scene this way:

Approaching a crowded office in the coastal
town of Capernaum, Jesus stares in sorrow at
the sinful ways of a tax collector named Levi
(aka Matthew — see Matthew 9:9). The Holy
One gazes down on the unholy tax man and
calls him to a life of holy rigor. And something
breaks in the heart of that sinful tax collector,
and he does a moral 180, as he rises from his
seat of iniquity to walk the aisle and follow
Jesus.

Maybe that rendition is the right one. Or maybe not.
What if, when Jesus tells Levi, "Follow me," he is not so
much offering a moral command but an escape hatch to

someone trapped in a life of greed and un-fulfillment? What if "follow me" is more like what a firefighter might say to a fearful victim trapped in a burning building? What if the subsequent party at Levi's house is truly a celebration for survivors rescued from disaster, or for sick sinners at last receiving sought-after medicine?

Jesus, keep showing us the escape hatch
of your mercy.

THE FATAL FLAW IN
COMPETITIVE RELIGION
(LUKE 5:33-39)

33 They said to him, "John's disciples often fast and pray, and so do the disciples of the Pharisees, but yours go on eating and drinking." 34 Jesus answered, "Can you make the friends of the bridegroom fast while he is with them? 35 But the time will come when the bridegroom will be taken from them; in those days they will fast."

As a pastor, I frequently meet guests who like much about our church but are nevertheless concerned about one key area where we are badly mistaken. A couple of weeks ago, it was that we do not use the King James Bible as our official translation. Others worry that we are not sufficiently patriotic enough on Fourth of July weekends.

It is oddly comforting for me to realize that even Jesus dealt with criticisms from people who found him religiously deficient. In the arena of competitive religion, Jesus' team came up short. His critics compared the laxity of Jesus's disciples to the scrupulousness of his cousin John the Baptist and also to the rigor of Pharisees like themselves. As far as these critics were concerned, Jesus's disciples were much more accomplished at eating and boozing it up than they were with disciplines like fasting and prayer.

Jesus (whose life, by the way, was one uninterrupted prayer) found their criticisms to be an excellent pretext for teaching about true religion. A faith of all fasting and no feasting is suspect. A faith with no room for the new and joyous wine of the gospel will eventually burst apart at the seams.

Jesus, give us wineskins fit for the new wine of the gospel.

RECEIVING GIFTS,
NOT ABUSING THEM
(LUKE 6:1-5)

¹ One Sabbath Jesus was going through the grainfields, and his disciples began to pick some heads of grain, rub them in their hands and eat the kernels. ² Some of the Pharisees asked, "Why are you doing what is unlawful on the Sabbath?" ³ Jesus answered them, "Have you never read what David did when he and his companions were hungry?"

If one day you brought me a costly housewarming gift—say, a beautiful crystal vase—and the next time you showed up at my house you noticed it carelessly filled with scissors and screwdrivers on a shelf in the corner, how would you feel? Angry, probably, since you paid a lot of money for that vase. Deeply confused, too, because I obviously completely misunderstood the nature and purpose of the gift.

As Chapter 6 opens, while Jesus' disciples are satisfying their hunger on a Sabbath walk by popping wheat kernels into their mouths like sunflower seeds, the Pharisees throw a penalty flag. They show that sad theological tendency to take a gift from God—a "Sabbath," a merciful break from the monotony of ceaseless work—and turn it into a new kind of onerous religious work.

A beautiful gift has been cheapened and put at risk by people who fail to understand its beauty and worth.

Jesus, a brilliant debater as well as preacher, points these Biblical scholars back to King David, who once grabbed some Sabbath loaves off the table in the Tabernacle to feed his starving companions (1 Samuel 21:6). David was never punished for doing so. Apparently, God's heart is on the side of the hungry, whether of body or soul. The Sabbath, Jesus assures us, was crafted to become not a terrible burden but a beautiful gift!

*Jesus, help us to receive your beautiful gifts
simply and gratefully.*

DEBATING THE GREAT DEBATER
(LUKE 6:6-11)

> *⁹ Then Jesus said to them, "I ask you, which is lawful on the Sabbath: to do good or to do evil, to save life or to destroy it?" ¹⁰ He looked around at them all, and then said to the man, "Stretch out your hand." He did so, and his hand was completely restored. ¹¹ But the Pharisees and the teachers of the law were furious and began to discuss with one another what they might do to Jesus.*

I was a member of a ninth-grade debating team. We created a variety of three-by-five cards with views on leading ethical issues of the day. The challenge, however, was that we would not know which side, "For" or "Against," was ours until fifteen minutes prior to the actual debate. The advantage of this method was that it helped us develop strong rhetorical skills. The disadvantage? It fostered an unintended cynicism. We were activists for hire, so to speak. *You choose the moral conviction, and we'll make it happen.*

This may be too strong an indictment of the Pharisees in this passage; these men obviously possessed strong feelings about the Sabbath. Still, Luke informs us that their driving motivation is not ethical or theological but personal: they were "looking for a reason to accuse Jesus…" (v. 7). You know you're in problematic territory when another man's healing becomes your opportunity for accusation.

Still, if you are going to debate Jesus, you need to realize that he has read all your notecards before the debate begins (v. 8). And if you want to make an argument *against* someone who would "save life" (v. 9), good luck! You see, the One who stands before you, the One who not only gives this reckless command to "stretch out your hand" but also has the incomparable power to heal it, will always be on the side of saving life, restoring life, even bringing life back from the dead—even if he has to give His own life to accomplish it.

Jesus, restore my withered faith in your
healing love.

THE JESUS DRAFT
(LUKE 6:12-16)

¹² One of those days Jesus went out to a mountainside to pray, and spent the night praying to God. ¹³ When morning came, he called his disciples to him and chose twelve of them, whom he also designated apostles: ¹⁴ Simon (whom he named Peter), his brother Andrew, James, John, Philip, Bartholomew, ¹⁵ Matthew, Thomas, James son of Alphaeus, Simon who was called the Zealot, ¹⁶ Judas son of James, and Judas Iscariot, who became a traitor.

Most of us typically end a prayer with an *Amen*, but Jesus ends his all-night vigil with a call to action. He summons twelve men to his side (and any Jewish listener could not fail to notice the mathematical harmony with the twelve tribes of Israel). How must it have felt to hear *your name* called? The vocal sounding of each name—"Simon," "Andrew," "James," etc.—was for each man the first domino to tip. Soon they would become friends, and friends would become pupils, and most of these pupils would become teachers. Indeed, they would be more than teachers. They would become Jesus' first carrier pigeons to transport the gospel across the world.

The plan looks good on paper. But did you see the guys Jesus chose? Fishermen? A tax collector? A zealot and a traitor? It seems like Jesus will call just about any-one.

My sons like to study "drafts" for professional sports leagues. They analyze the needs of their favorite teams and the best available collegiate athletes to fill those spots. There is surely a science and an art to it all. But Jesus has apparently thrown this kind of worldly wis-dom out the window. He is unconcerned with our skill. He has enough of that for all of us.

Jesus, let us hear your call to us today.

SALVE FOR STEPPED-ON TOES
(LUKE 6:17-26)

> [17] *"He went down with them and stood on a level place. A large crowd of his disciples was there and a great number of people from all over Judea, from Jerusalem, and from the coastal region around Tyre and Sidon,* [18] *who had come to hear him and to be healed of their diseases. Those troubled by impure spirits were cured,* [19] *and the people all tried to touch him, because power was coming from him and healing them all.* [20] *Looking at his disciples, he said: "Blessed are you who are poor, for yours is the kingdom of God."*

There's a curious assessment that people in my part of the Christian world often make about preachers. "I like our pastor, Brother Fred," they might say. "I like his sermons...he really knows how to *step on your toes*." I think I understand what they're meaning. Good preaching humbles us with the law (that's the part that gets uncomfortably close to our toes), so that it might lift us up with the word of grace. Ultimately, though, what our souls need most is not more bruised toes. Life tends to do a good deal more bruising than we would prefer.

What we need is for Jesus to descend from his prayer retreat in the mountains and bring his grace to us. We need whatever healing he has to spare for broken bodies and troubled minds (vv. 18-19). And that is precisely what Jesus does. He seems incapable of restraining the gracious power that springs out from him (v. 19).

And still, Jesus is not done. He brings out dessert trays of blessings to all those whom life has deeply wounded—the poor and hungry, the grieving and persecuted. The only people who receive the lumps of coal (vv. 24-26) are those whose hands and stomachs are already full of the world's junk food. All they get is the "woe" of missing out on grace completely.

Jesus, may your power heal
our bruises today (v. 19).

CAN JESUS DEFINE "ENEMY"?
(LUKE 6:27-36)

> [27] *"But to you who are listening I say: Love your enemies, do good to those who hate you,* [28] *bless those who curse you, pray for those who mistreat you.* [29] *If someone slaps you on one cheek, turn to them the other also. If someone takes your coat, do not withhold your shirt from them.* [30] *Give to everyone who asks you, and if anyone takes what belongs to you, do not demand it back.* [31] *Do to others as you would have them do to you.*

These words are written only to those "who are listening" (v. 27). To someone outside the Christian faith, they may sound nonsensical, comical, or worse. As I read them again, they bring me to my knees, subverting the very definition of an "enemy" (someone I hate). In rapid succession, Jesus instructs me to love them, do tangible good for them, bless them and even pray for them, to turn my un-struck cheek in the direction of a slap, and to freely offer a gift to their dirty, thieving hands. What madness! I mean, I'm fine in theory with the "golden rule" (v. 31), but not when it comes to my enemies.

If that's not bad enough, Jesus exposes what passes for love in my life. Too much of what I label love in my relationships he sees as bartering and back scratching.

My kindness is roughly equivalent to *good business*, more strategic than selfless.

It makes me think of that Lyle Lovett song, "God Will," where the singer asks his unfaithful lover who will forgive her and trust her again and keep on loving her?

"God does / But I don't / God will / But I won't / And that's the difference / Between God and me."

Only Jesus can truly love an enemy. Only Jesus has done this (Romans 5:10). And if you ever see anything close to something like this happening anywhere close to me, you know that somehow Jesus' Spirit has snuck into my body and, against all odds, has done it again.

Jesus, you turn enemies into friends.

THE BENEFIT OF
HALF-CLOSED EYES
(LUKE 6:37-42)

39 He also told them this parable: "Can the blind lead the blind? Will they not both fall into a pit? 40 The student is not above the teacher, but everyone who is fully trained will be like their teacher. 41 "Why do you look at the speck of sawdust in your brother's eye and pay no attention to the plank in your own eye? 42 How can you say to your brother, 'Brother, let me take the speck out of your eye,' when you yourself fail to see the plank in your own eye? You hypocrite, first take the plank out of your eye, and then you will see clearly to remove the speck from your brother's eye.

One of my wife's favorite quotes to contribute to a wedding shower, when the hosts solicit the best advice guests can offer the future bride and groom, goes something like this: "Keep your eyes wide open before marriage, and half-shut after." Pretty good advice, isn't it? If we intend marriage to last a lifetime, we should choose a mate wisely. But once the choice is made, that same discerning eye can be counterproductive if it continues to identify minor faults from fifty yards.

Judgment—such a good quality when selecting cantaloupe at a farmer's market or choosing a candidate for an open position—becomes deadly in our deepest relationships. As it turns out, there is always something defective in the people who surround us. Don't look too hard, or you will surely find it.

What is more, the very people who grab tweezers to pluck the faults from the eyes of others are in danger of misunderstanding their own moral corruption (not to mention that the Christian faith is built on grace and not moral perfection). The pride at the heart of our hypocrisy not only sets a terrible example (v. 39). It produces bad fruit (v. 43) and leaves a flimsy foundation upon which to build a life (vv. 46-49).

Jesus, you pour so much grace into our unde-serving laps (v. 38).

WHEN EVEN JESUS IS
ASTOUNDED
(LUKE 7:1-10)

⁶ So Jesus went with them. He was not far from the house when the centurion sent friends to say to him: "Lord, don't trouble yourself, for I do not deserve to have you come under my roof.
⁷ That is why I did not even consider myself worthy to come to you. But say the word, and my servant will be healed. ⁸ For I myself am a man under authority, with soldiers under me. I tell this one, 'Go,' and he goes; and that one, 'Come,' and he comes. I say to my servant, 'Do this,' and he does it." ⁹ When Jesus heard this, he was amazed at him, and turning to the crowd following him, he said, "I tell you, I have not found such great faith even in Israel."

This centurion defies our preconceptions. He must be an impressive man to rise to rule over a company of one hundred Roman soldiers. A hardened and battle-tested commander, he still has a tender spot in his heart for a highly-valued and desperately ill servant. We would assume that Jewish elders would be predisposed to hate a man who wears the uniform of their oppressors; still, this centurion had actually built a synagogue for them!

For these reasons, we would surely want to enjoy a meal with this guy.

Jesus finds a deeper reason to note the centurion's character—his humility (v. 7) combined with faith. This powerful Roman commander "gets" authority. He knows that when a powerful person speaks the right "word," in the right place, that word becomes reality. The centurion has watched that happen many times. But he intuits that Jesus is authoritative over a much larger domain.

Jesus is astounded by that man's faith. I can see him jerking a thumb in the direction of the centurion and saying, "Can you believe this guy? I've been a lot of places and never seen a guy 'get it' like he gets it."

Do you get it? If so, your unworthiness before Jesus is no barrier. Just ask Him to say the word—the word of forgiveness, the word of grace, the word that heals what deeply ails us.

Jesus, just say the word.

STOP THAT FUNERAL!
(LUKE 7:11-17)

12 As he approached the town gate, a dead person was being carried out—the only son of his mother, and she was a widow. And a large crowd from the town was with her. 13 When the Lord saw her, his heart went out to her and he said, "Don't cry." 14 Then he went up and touched the bier they were carrying him on, and the bearers stood still. He said, "Young man, I say to you, get up!"

As a pastor officiating a funeral, I am always grateful for the partnership of a good funeral director. They know how to take charge at the hardest moments, like leading the pallbearers up the hill from the casket to the graveside, or asking the grieving family to crowd under the awning. So I'm wondering how the Nain Funeral Home director responded when Jesus walked right up to the funeral procession and brought it to a standstill? When Jesus told a widow who had just lost everything—her only son, her financial security, her status—"Don't cry"? When Jesus *touched* the casket, becoming ritually unclean himself? When he spoke to the corpse? Seasoned funeral directors have seen everything (I mean *everything*). Crazy stuff happens at funerals. But no funeral director in Nain's long history had ever seen this.

Today's entrepreneurs like to throw around the word "disruptor," as in, Uber disrupting the taxi business. Jesus is clearly disrupting the death business—not the finances of death but the reality of death. If his deep compassion (v. 13) and incomparable power can reverse a funeral procession, if he can make dead men talk (v. 15), then we are seeing much more than a "great prophet" (v. 16). If he can give grieving mothers back their sons, what can't he give?

Jesus, you traded your death that our deaths
may be gloriously disrupted.

NOT QUITE WHAT
WE EXPECTED
(LUKE 7:18-23)

> *[20] When the men came to Jesus, they said, "John the Baptist sent us to you to ask, 'Are you the one who is to come, or should we expect someone else?'" [21] At that very time Jesus cured many who had diseases, sicknesses and evil spirits, and gave sight to many who were blind. [22] So he replied to the messengers, "Go back and report to John what you have seen and heard: The blind receive sight, the lame walk, those who have leprosy are cleansed, the deaf hear, the dead are raised, and the good news is proclaimed to the poor. [23] Blessed is anyone who does not stumble on account of me."*

Sometimes, when a group is trying to hire someone, different visions float around a single room. *Let's get a strategist*, thinks one frustrated strategic thinker. *We need someone who can tell it like it is*, muses the lone outspoken person in the room. *We will fail if we don't get someone with good people skills*, thinks the resident touchy-feely. Everyone has their own unofficial profile for this new hire.

John the Baptist, stymied in prison, might have expected the real Messiah to be a little more in-your-face

—an ax-swinger and a fire-starter (Luke 3:9). But Jesus' messianic campaign is not proceeding exactly how John imagined. So John sends two of his own men to ask a delicate question: "Jesus, your excellency, I know I said all those nice things about you prior to your baptism. Just double checking to make sure you are the Messiah we prayed for. If not, no problem, we'll just keep waiting."

John likely missed the sermon (Luke 4:18-19), but Jesus had already told us what kind of Messiah he would be. He is not here to be anybody's perfect candidate. He is here to do what the Spirit of the Lord anointed him to do, which is to apply his grace to wounded eyes and ears and legs and lives and souls. And, if we might paraphrase verse 23, "Blessed is the one who is willing to scrap their messianic profile to let Jesus be Jesus."

Jesus, open our blind eyes to your
true identity today.

THE LAST OF HIS KIND
(LUKE 7:23-35)

26 "But what did you go out to see? A prophet? Yes, I tell you, and more than a prophet. 27 This is the one about whom it is written: 'I will send my messenger ahead of you, who will prepare your way before you.' 28 I tell you, among those born of women there is no one greater than John; yet the one who is least in the kingdom of God is greater than he."

So, what are we to make of John the Baptist? How does Jesus explain John's legacy? Jesus begins with what feels like a premature eulogy. John defied the expectations of his hearers—a sturdy and popular prophet who kept himself pure from corrupting influences of power. Still, as highly as Jesus praises his forerunner, he also makes clear that John was the last of his kind. *John, the last of an old age, was a great man, make no mistake about it; but you, people of my new kingdom, have a power far greater available to you.*

Jesus wants his disciples leaning forward, ready to receive the wisdom he offers. This requires the faith John models, not the cynicism of the Pharisees and law experts (v. 30). They have revealed themselves to be spoiled Goldilocks—*John the Baptist was too ascetic*, they claimed, while *Jesus is too much of a libertine.*

As we stand among the crowd, can we marvel at the way God drops prophets into our lives to inspire and warn us? Even more, can we allow John to continue to point us toward the only one who can fill us with the greatness of His grace (v. 28)?

Jesus, you are the Wisdom of God (v. 35).

THE GOSPEL FOR THE
FLAT BROKE
(LUKE 7:36-50)

*³⁶ When one of the Pharisees invited Jesus to
have dinner with him, he went to the Pharisee's
house and reclined at the table. ³⁷ A woman in
that town who lived a sinful life learned that
Jesus was eating at the Pharisee's house, so she
came there with an alabaster jar of perfume.
³⁸ As she stood behind him at his feet weeping,
she began to wet his feet with her tears. Then
she wiped them with her hair, kissed them and
poured perfume on them.*

This passage reads like a set of nesting dolls. Think of
the outer doll as a respectable religious dinner party.
Jesus, invited to the home of a Pharisee named Simon,
must feel a bit on edge, like when you are treated to a
fancy meal by a fierce critic.

Inside the dinner scene, we happen upon a moment
of deep social embarrassment—a woman who has lived
a "sinful life" has infiltrated the bulwark of respectabil-
ity and broken every known rule of decorum. Her very
presence is unwelcome, and she makes it worse by weeping, smashing a valuable heirloom, and turning Jesus'
feet into a sticky mess of perfume and tears.

And inside the awkwardness of that situation, Jesus nests a parable about two debtors, one less-broke and the other more-broke, but both flat broke. He is trying to open Simon's spiritually blind eyes to his own inner poverty and need for grace.

And then, at the center of this stunning meal are those beautiful words, spoken over the woman who worships at Jesus' feet. *Your sins are forgiven...Your faith* (itself a gift of grace) *has saved you...Walk in the peace I now give you.*

> *Jesus, may we uncover your forgiveness and*
> *peace at the center of our chaos today.*

JESUS' WHISTLE-STOP TOUR
(LUKE 8:1-3)

> *[1] After this, Jesus traveled about from one town and village to another, proclaiming the good news of the kingdom of God. The Twelve were with him, [2] and also some women who had been cured of evil spirits and diseases: Mary (called Magdalene) from whom seven demons had come out; [3] Joanna the wife of Chuza, the manager of Herod's household; Susanna; and many others. These women were helping to support them out of their own means.*

A hundred years ago, it was not uncommon for a political candidate to board a train and commence a "whistle stop" campaign. I can almost hear those trains as I read this passage. Yes, the locomotion is by foot rather than train, but Jesus is clearly the candidate at the center of the commotion. His platform is the "good news" of his kingdom. It is not surprising to see Jesus' twelve (male) disciples on the "train" with him. What startles us are the women on board the Jesus train—women whom Jesus has *cured*.

Look at Mary Magdalene, freed of seven—count them—*seven*—demons! And now, she is a part of his campaign. Did you see Joanna? Does King Herod know she's here? And Susanna? They too travel through the towns and villages with Jesus, supporting him out of whatever handsome or limited funds are made available to them.

My friends, marvel at the grace that not only cures us but also *calls* us to become workers and investors in Jesus' campaign. Look at these women—each one with her own story. Watch them walking, trampling over demons in the dust.

> *Jesus, your grace not only saves us but quali-*
> *fies us to work on your campaign.*

A DOCUMENTARY ON SEEDS
(LUKE 8:4-15)

> [5] *"A farmer went out to sow his seed. As he was scattering the seed, some fell along the path; it was trampled on, and the birds ate it up.* [6] *Some fell on rocky ground, and when it came up, the plants withered because they had no moisture.* [7] *Other seed fell among thorns, which grew up with it and choked the plants.* [8] *Still other seed fell on good soil. It came up and yielded a crop, a hundred times more than was sown." When he said this, he called out, "Whoever has ears to hear, let them hear."*

This parable, told as large numbers of onlookers are crowding around Jesus, provides a physical picture of the spiritual realities represented in their hearts.

You could read this parable as one of those obscure public-television nature documentaries, this one on the inside story of seeds. In one scene, we watch clumps of seeds falling along the cart path and becoming cheap snack food for the Devil. In another, we see those seeds half-buried in gravel sprout vulnerable plants which wither away in hard times. And then we watch those seeds which have the misfortune of fighting for moisture among the weeds (this scene frightens me the most—those seeds that fall among "life's worries, riches, and pleasures" (v. 14). When a time-lapse video shows that seed springing up from good soil, we stifle a cheer in our hearts. We sense nothing less than a miracle when Jesus cleans a heart and plants a seed that produces an unlikely harvest.

Then Jesus interrupts his documentary with a strangely shouted command (or is it an anguish cry?): "Whoever has ears to hear, let them hear" (v. 8). Jesus knows that his parables function like revolving doors, hurling deep listeners toward him while flinging the hard of hearing farther away.

What are we to make of this? Are the soils *people*? I think they better represent seasons in our lives where we are unreceptive or receptive to Christ's generous presence. Personally, the parable frightens me *and* motivates me to pray for grace to sink down deep within my heart.

Jesus, open our ears and hearts
to the seed of your word.

PUTTING HIS WORDS
INTO PLAY
(LUKE 8:16-21)

16 "No one lights a lamp and hides it in a clay jar or puts it under a bed. Instead, they put it on a stand, so that those who come in can see the light. 17 For there is nothing hidden that will not be disclosed, and nothing concealed that will not be known or brought out into the open. 18 Therefore consider carefully how you listen. Whoever has will be given more; whoever does not have, even what they think they have will be taken from them."

My wife likes to tease me about something that happened on our honeymoon. We walked into a casino in the Bahamas, a first time for both of us. She wanted to put just one quarter in a slot machine, but I asked her not to do so. A Baptist seminarian at the time, I did not feel good about investing even twenty-five cents in that morally dubious industry.

So I'm surprised as anyone to conclude that in this passage rich with images—lanterns and clay jars, the damp dark beneath the bed and the airy light at the top of the lampstand—what sticks out to me most is Jesus at the roulette table.

Okay, yes, Jesus is not literally at a roulette table. But ponder again these daring words: "Whoever has will be given more; whoever does not have, even what they think they have will be taken from them" (v. 18). I hear Jesus saying that whoever puts his words into play will see a big payoff—including becoming his fully-fledged family members (v. 21)! Meanwhile, those risk-adverse folk who conceal Jesus' words like pocket change will soon discover a hole in their pockets when they get back home.

Jesus, let your words loose in my life.

HAVE YOU NOT BEEN PAYING ATTENTION? (LUKE 8:22-25)

> *²³ As they sailed, he fell asleep. A squall came down on the lake, so that the boat was being swamped, and they were in great danger. ²⁴ The disciples went and woke him, saying, "Master, Master, we're going to drown!" He got up and rebuked the wind and the raging waters; the storm subsided, and all was calm. ²⁵ "Where is your faith?" he asked his disciples. In fear and amazement they asked one another, "Who is this? He commands even the winds and the water, and they obey him."*

So far in this chapter, Jesus makes some pretty audacious claims about his *words*. These words, like seeds on good soil, have the potential of producing a crop of "a hundred times more than was sown" (v. 8). Since his words are so valuable, we should listen "carefully," and are assured that those who pay close attention to them will be given more (v. 18). We've even heard Jesus say that those who "hear" and "practice" God's word are made a part of his family (v. 21)!

But do the disciples "hear" and "practice" Jesus' words? Do we? When the fierce storm is swamping the boat, have the words that Christ has spoken taken deep enough root in our hearts to calm the inner squall (v. 13)? Probably not. Our faith knows enough to call him "Master, Master," but our fear predicts that drowning is imminent (v. 24).

Thankfully, Jesus is so patient to speak those chaos-defying words over the "raging waters." In response, all the disciples can seem to mutter is the question everyone wrestles with in this gospel: "Who is this?"

Jesus, may your words rouse
our moribund faith.

A GOSPEL FOR THE OTHER SIDE
(LUKE 8:26-39)

> *35 And the people went out to see what had happened. When they came to Jesus, they found the man from whom the demons had gone out, sitting at Jesus' feet, dressed and in his right mind; and they were afraid. 36 Those who had seen it told the people how the demon-possessed man had been cured. 37 Then all the people of the region of the Gerasenes asked Jesus to leave them, because they were overcome with fear. So he got into the boat and left.*

It is one thing for the gospel to work in the carefully controlled conditions of Sunday School—where all our chairs are set neatly in a circle, coffee and danishes arranged attractively on the counter, and we are outfitted in our Sunday best with our Bibles held securely in our hands. But what if we take the gospel to the *other side* of the lake, among all those pigs and tomb-dwellers? Will the gospel still work in the Hell outside the city limits?

It will, but only because Jesus stands amidst the chaos. This is no "gentle Jesus meek and mild." Jesus is pulling demons over on the side of the highway, taking their drivers' licenses, and incarcerating them at the bottom of the sea.

If you want to know if his gospel "works" in a hostile environment, notice first how many people are struck by it. More importantly, note carefully the before-and-after condition of the formerly demonized man. Gone are his tremors, his nakedness, his chains, his screams, and his pitiful isolation. Now, we see him clothed and at peace, "sitting at Jesus' feet" (code words designating a true disciple). Jesus even sends the man home to be a missionary (v. 39).

Jesus, you boldly bring light to
the darkest places.

THE SIGNAL AND THE NOISE
(LUKE 8:40-56)

> *[44] She came up behind him and touched the edge of his cloak, and immediately her bleeding stopped. [45] "Who touched me?" Jesus asked. When they all denied it, Peter said, "Master, the people are crowding and pressing against you." [46] But Jesus said, "Someone touched me; I know that power has gone out from me." [47] Then the woman, seeing that she could not go unnoticed, came trembling and fell at his feet. In the presence of all the people, she told why she had touched him and how she had been instantly healed. [48] Then he said to her, "Daughter, your faith has healed you. Go in peace."*

The gospel of Luke doesn't come with a soundtrack, but with this passage we don't need one. It does not take much imagination to hear the roar of the crowd waiting for Jesus when he steps off the boat (v. 40), the shouts of Jairus imploring Jesus to visit the sickbed of his daughter (v. 42), the white noise of people "crowding and pressing" against Jesus (v. 45), and the haunting "wailing and mourning" when Jairus's sick daughter dies (v. 52). We not only hear this text, we *feel* it. We feel knocked involuntarily from one foot to the other as the sweaty bodies jostle us and shove us off course. At some point, in the sensory overload, we stop hearing and feeling altogether.

But not Jesus. He manages to signal private, healing words in the middle of the chaos. He *hears* Jairus's pleas and *feels* the touch of a hopelessly sick woman (whom he both heals and blesses). He silences the cries of the mourners (v. 52). He speaks tenderly to lifeless ears and grasps the lifeless hand of Jairus's daughter to lift her back onto her feet.

This passage fills me with the absurd hope that in the blaring noise and suffering in this life, Jesus tunes into our cries and feels our grasping hands and sends His power into us, too.

Jesus, signal your peace in the middle
of our noise.

UNPACKING OUR SUITCASES
(LUKE 9:1-9)

> *¹ When Jesus had called the Twelve together, he gave them power and authority to drive out all demons and to cure diseases, ² and he sent them out to proclaim the kingdom of God and to heal the sick. ³ He told them: "Take nothing for the journey—no staff, no bag, no bread, no money, no extra shirt. ⁴ Whatever house you enter, stay there until you leave that town.*

I still remember my embarrassment while preparing to embark on a church trip to South America. My companions each rolled up with their compact carry-ons while I was dragging this gigantic red suitcase. I had packed for every possible contingency—excess clothes and medicines and creature comforts to hedge against my anxiety about the austere culture I would soon visit.

Jesus takes austerity to a whole new level. Essentially, he starts *unpacking* items from his disciples' suitcases—necessities like food and money and clothes and even the suitcases themselves! As best I can tell, all Jesus would allow his disciples to take with them was his "power and authority" (v. 1) and his good news about God's Kingdom (v. 2). Everything else they needed would be provided for them on the road.

Even the mighty Herod would get word of their gospel preaching and healing miracles. Herod, who has by now beheaded John the Baptist, is convinced that Jesus is either John or someone long dead, who has come back to life. As the disciples shared the good news, the fragrance of Resurrection was in the air, and even a corrupt murderer like Herod could smell it.

Jesus, teach us not to leave home without the fragrance of your Resurrection.

HIDDEN ABUNDANCE
(LUKE 9:10-17)

[12] Late in the afternoon the Twelve came to him and said, "Send the crowd away so they can go to the surrounding villages and countryside and find food and lodging, because we are in a remote place here." [13] He replied, "You give them something to eat." They answered, "We have only five loaves of bread and two fish—unless we go and buy food for all this crowd." [14] (About five thousand men were there.) But he said to his disciples, "Have them sit down in groups of about fifty each."

Near the center of this passage are two words which are the fulcrum of this miracle: *"You give..."* Could such words arrive at a more inconvenient time?

The disciples begin the day with a *good-kind-of-tired*. They have just returned from a mission trip and have powerful miracles to report to Jesus. Their reward? Jesus is taking them to Bethsaida for a little rest and relaxation. But pesky crowds hear about it (v. 11) and surprise them at the dock. The disciples watch Jesus do what Jesus typically does—he welcomes and teaches and heals. But enough is enough—the people need to go find food, and the disciples need a break—*for the people's sake, Lord, send them away.* But instead, Jesus tells the beyond-tired disciples to give a little more—of their food and time and energy and faith. Flabbergasted, they reluctantly obey, only to watch Jesus perform a quiet miracle of multiplication so noteworthy that all four gospel writers record it.

"You give." Jesus chooses to channel his lavish abundance during hours when his disciples are beyond empty.

Jesus, multiply yourself in our fatigue.

TRUE HOPE GOES DOWN
WITH THE SHIP
(LUKE 9:18-27)

²² And he said, "The Son of Man must suffer many things and be rejected by the elders, the chief priests and the teachers of the law, and he must be killed and on the third day be raised to life." ²³ Then he said to them all: "Whoever wants to be my disciple must deny themselves and take up their cross daily and follow me. ²⁴ For whoever wants to save their life will lose it, but whoever loses their life for me will save it."

This is a story about one "who" and many "whoevers." The "who" refers to Jesus' true identity—an issue of great confusion among his contemporaries and our contemporaries. Jesus asks *who* the crowds say he is and Peter luckily gets the answer right. Jesus is not just one more in a class of noteworthy prophets (vv. 19-20). He is not *a* mere prophet; he is *the* Messiah. Still, his disciples will need to learn that the true Messiah is the suffering Messiah.

The dark notes of suffering continue: The "whoevers," those who wish to follow Jesus, only truly understand Jesus and themselves through a lens of loss then gain, suffering then resurrection. But who wants that?

Who wants to "lose their life" (v. 24)? Who wants to follow a Loser?

Thomas Merton, a Trappist monk, drew inspiration from the Desert Fathers and Mothers, pilgrims from the early centuries of church history who sought Christ's presence in the austerity of the wilderness. In *The Wisdom of the Desert*, he wrote that they regarded the world as a "shipwreck from which each single individual man had to swim for his life." Those pilgrims witnessed a truth we often miss. Even our "best life" is taking on water and bound to capsize sooner than later. Our best and, indeed, only hope is found when our "best life" capsizes. Only then do we discover the Risen One who awaits us on the shore.

Jesus, keep our eyes focused
on the third day (v. 22).

TRY SAYING NOTHING
(LUKE 9:28-36)

29 As he was praying, the appearance of his face changed, and his clothes became as bright as a flash of lightning. 30 Two men, Moses and Elijah, appeared in glorious splendor, talking with Jesus. 31 They spoke about his departure, which he was about to bring to fulfillment at Jerusalem. 32 Peter and his companions were very sleepy, but when they became fully awake, they saw his glory and the two men standing with him.

Preachers often rip Peter for the impulsive things he does and says, including his offer (v. 33) to build three shelters for Jesus and the two Old Testament worthies who shared his moment of transfiguration. But really, what would you say in that moment?

I mean, say you're Peter. You and your companions James and John are tired out from a hike up a mountain with Jesus, so you take a little nap. When you wake, Jesus is practically on fire, while two of your greatest heroes of the faith are talking with Jesus about his coming *departure*, and you are going to say something profound? You are going to make meaning of all this? Of course Peter "did not know what he was saying" (v. 33)!

In such beautifully transfigured moments, silence is golden. There will be time later to reconcile so many Old Covenant themes—the mountain, the lightning, the glowing, Moses and Elijah, and the descending cloud of God's presence—with the New Covenant Jesus is bringing. Now is not that time. For now, as God instructs, we simply bask in the loveliness of Jesus. Now is the time to "listen" (v. 35).

Jesus, you are God's Beloved.

A BROKEN HEART ON DISPLAY
(LUKE 9:37-42)

[39] "A spirit seizes him and he suddenly screams; it throws him into convulsions so that he foams at the mouth. It scarcely ever leaves him and is destroying him. [40] I begged your disciples to drive it out, but they could not." [41] "You unbelieving and perverse generation," Jesus replied, "how long shall I stay with you and put up with you? Bring your son here." [42] Even while the boy was coming, the demon threw him to the ground in a convulsion. But Jesus rebuked the impure spirit, healed the boy and gave him back to his father.

Jesus' broken, angry heart is here on display. His heart sprints to those under Satan's grip, like this poor boy, helpless in Satan's hands, seizing and convulsing and involuntarily screaming at the destructive power of evil. Jesus' heart is pierced by the desperate voice of the boy's father begging anyone who can to do something for his "only child." And then to see these disciples whom earlier in this chapter Jesus equipped with power to drive out demons (v. 1), standing around with their hands in their tunics? It is as if his disciples have forgotten the combination to the lock to Jesus' medicine cabinet.

Jesus funnels his holy rage into a cry of rebuke, a rearguard attack on the forces that attack the defenseless boy. He then gives a brokenhearted father the best gift he could ever receive: his healed son back in his arms at last.

I'll say it. I am skittish about the anger Jesus vents on his disciples. But am I as uncomfortable as Jesus is with faithlessness, and with the evil that is regularly let loose among us?

Jesus, your anger toward evil is justified.

ADVENTURES IN
MIS-TRANSLATION
(LUKE 9:43-50)

⁴⁵ But they did not understand what this meant. It was hidden from them, so that they did not grasp it, and they were afraid to ask him about it. ⁴⁶ An argument started among the disciples as to which of them would be the greatest. ⁴⁷ Jesus, knowing their thoughts, took a little child and had him stand beside him.

My friend John speaks excellent German, and when he and I were in Berlin I let him lead the way through social encounters. A woman approached us at a crowded thoroughfare, evidently needing directions. John spoke first German and then English to her but little connection was made. I made a quick cultural assessment and threw out a few Spanish words, and the woman quickly responded. The three of us actually had a good laugh about our linguistic misadventures.

That memory comes to mind as I try to make sense of the incomprehension taking place in this passage. Jesus speaks one language, trying to prep his disciples for the cross that lies ahead. But like a Spanish-speaker hearing German, the disciples were completely mystified. They could not "grasp" his painful truth and were afraid even to try (v. 45). Instead, they shouted in their native dialects of rivalry (v. 46) and exclusion (v. 49).

Jesus, desperate to communicate, points to a child. *My people* (he says with his arms around someone no one had noticed) *include, not exclude. We revel in the insignificant; we do not fight over significance.* And Jesus' disciples, then and now, say, "Huh?"

Jesus, speak slowly and clearly again
to us today.

ON THE ROAD WITH JESUS

(LUKE 9:51-22:71)

What do I miss most when I'm away from home? I'm tempted to say my pillow, which is thinner and softer and more moldable than the average hotel pillow. I am also quite partial to my worn spot on the edge of the sofa, and the end table where I lay my coffee cup and books in the mornings. Oh, and perhaps I should have first mentioned my family! As much as I love the comforts of home, nothing is harder than airport good-byes.

As Jesus "resolutely set out for Jerusalem" (Luke 9:51), he possessed no comforts from home—especially not the comfort of family. He memorably tells us that while "foxes have dens and birds have nests," he has "no place to lay his head" (9:58). As we accompany Jesus on his arduous journey to Jerusalem, as what awaits him dawns on us, can we feel the urgency of the journey and the sacrifices he will make to ensure that we will be adopted into God's home?

WALKING AN IMPOSSIBLE LINE
(LUKE 9:51-56)

> *51 As the time approached for him to be taken up to heaven, Jesus resolutely set out for Jerusalem. 52 And he sent messengers on ahead, who went into a Samaritan village to get things ready for him; 53 but the people there did not welcome him, because he was heading for Jerusalem. 54 When the disciples James and John saw this, they asked, "Lord, do you want us to call fire down from heaven to destroy them?"*

I can remember Saturday nights watching TV with my dad in the early 1970s, when one of our musical heroes would take the stage and announce, "Hello, I'm Johnny Cash." The Man in Black would then launch into songs I could sing by heart yet was too young to understand. "Walk the Line" laid out his intentions for fidelity to his marriage vows; "Ring of Fire" described the ever-present temptation to fall into a burning and passionate affair.

Is it too odd to add these two songs to the soundtrack of this passage? Jesus sees that the *line* which will eventually take him back to his Father's side runs through Jerusalem's cross. He is resolute—like the prophet Isaiah, Jesus could say, "I have set my face like flint" (Isaiah 50:7). He will walk a line of dogged devotion to serve his bride, the Church (Ephesians 5:29).

The "ring of fire," on the other hand, is what those two combustible brothers, James and John, have in mind for their enemies. These two "sons of thunder" are filled with resentment that these hated Samaritans refused hospitality to Jesus. Like their hero Elijah in 1 Kings 18, they wish to engulf that Samaritan village in fiery judgment. But James and John, like us, can only watch as Jesus will complete his journey to Jerusalem and there reveal a love deep enough to endure the fire of judgment and swallow retribution.

Jesus, you walked a line of unquestioning fidelity to God and to us.

JESUS' PRESS SECRETARY
(LUKE 9:57-62)

[59] He said to another man, "Follow me." But [the man] replied, "Lord, first let me go and bury my father." [60] Jesus said to him, "Let the dead bury their own dead, but you go and proclaim the kingdom of God." [61] Still another said, "I will follow you, Lord; but first let me go back and say goodbye to my family." [62] Jesus replied, "No one who puts a hand to the plow and looks back is fit for service in the kingdom of God."

Sometimes, like Jesus' Press Secretary, I attempt to blunt the force of the controversial things Jesus says and does.

"Excuse me, Mr. Press Secretary, but does Jesus really tell a would-be follower that he could not take a day or two to bury his father first?" *Ahh, yes, well, I don't think we should twist Jesus' words to characterize Jesus as anti-burial or anything like that...*

"And what about telling someone else that he couldn't hug his family goodbye first? I mean, isn't it true that the Great Elijah allows his protege Elisha to settle his affairs first (1 Kings 19:19-21)?" *Well, now, I do see that on the surface it could appear a little rude, but you need to understand...*

While part of me wants to soften Jesus' words here, it might be better if we felt the full brunt of them. What if Jesus knows that, beneath excuses that seem legitimate on the surface, we are not truly ready to accompany him on the journey? To what degree do these excuses paper over our delay tactics when it comes to following Jesus? What if these impossibly strict warnings are there to destroy any self-confidence we might bring to Jesus?

Here's what I know: if my hand stays on the plow (v. 62), it is only because God's grace has glued it there!

Jesus, we thank you that you are ready for the journey even when we are not.

PLANTING PEACE IN A
CHAOTIC WORLD
(LUKE 10:1-24)

² He told them, "The harvest is plentiful, but the workers are few. Ask the Lord of the harvest, therefore, to send out workers into his harvest field. ³ Go! I am sending you out like lambs among wolves. ⁴ Do not take a purse or bag or sandals; and do not greet anyone on the road. ⁵ When you enter a house, first say, 'Peace to this house.'

Today's gospel reading is too long, isn't it? I had intended to parcel it out in smaller pieces. Still, I grew fascinated by the commissioning of thirty-six pairs of workers sent out to "harvest" new gospel believers. And then I feared that Jesus would practically talk them out of it before they ever got started, what with his "you will be like lambs among wolves" and "pack next to nothing" and "be prepared for outright rejection."

I wanted to cut off the reading right there (v. 11), but Jesus kept going, pleading with gospel-resistant cities like Capernaum to stop spurning the Kingdom message and receive the "peace" his disciples are bringing. And right about the time I thought we had reached a good stopping place, the 72 were back and jumping up and down over the fact that they had seen the demons tremble at Jesus' name. And in the next breath Jesus intimates he somehow mysteriously saw Satan's defeat playing out before his eyes.

Maybe this is what life is like on the road with Jesus—ample reasons not to go, but would you really want to miss out on all this excitement (v. 24)?

Jesus, let your good news keep nudging us forward.

GO AND DO LIKEWISE?
(LUKE 10:25-37)

[34] "He went to him and bandaged his wounds, pouring on oil and wine. Then he put the man on his own donkey, brought him to an inn and took care of him. [35] The next day he took out two denarii and gave them to the innkeeper. 'Look after him,' he said, 'and when I return, I will reimburse you for any extra expense you may have.' [36] Which of these three do you think was a neighbor to the man who fell into the hands of robbers?" [37] The expert in the law replied, "The one who had mercy on him." Jesus told him, "Go and do likewise."

Twice here Jesus tells a religious expert to do something impossible. After the expert recites the heart of the Law (to love God flawlessly and your neighbor sacrificially), Jesus says, "Do this, and you will live" (v. 28). Then, on the other side of this famous Good Samaritan parable of an outsider showing outrageous love to his cultural enemy, Jesus says, "Go and do likewise" (v. 37).

My problem? I know all too well that I cannot adequately accomplish what Jesus asks. My love for God is imperfect at best; like the expert in this passage, I am always looking to limit the extent of the love I show and the number of "neighbors" to whom I must show it.

But what if Jesus doesn't tell this story to lay down an impossible roadmap toward eternal life (a life that we can only "inherit" anyway, not earn)? What if, instead, Jesus wants us to see a picture of his mercy played out?

In Wendell Berry's short story, "The Hurt Man," five-year-old Mat watches his mother tend to a terribly wounded man who has run away from a drunken brawl. What young Mat sees in his mother's face "would remain with him forever. It was pity, but it was more than that. It was a hurt love that seemed to include entirely the hurt man. It included him and disregarded everything else...." Jesus, both Samaritan and Victim, demonstrates "hurt love" by becoming our "hurt man."

Jesus, you are our merciful neighbor.

WAITING ON WORDS
(LUKE 10:38-42)

38 As Jesus and his disciples were on their way, he came to a village where a woman named Martha opened her home to him. 39 She had a sister called Mary, who sat at the Lord's feet listening to what he said. 40 But Martha was distracted by all the preparations that had to be made. She came to him and asked, "Lord, don't you care that my sister has left me to do the work by myself? Tell her to help me!" 41 "Martha, Martha," the Lord answered, "you are worried and upset about many things, 42 but few things are needed—or indeed only one. Mary has chosen what is better, and it will not be taken away from her."

Those of us who are responsible for helping families—especially *church* families—function day by day might be tempted to hide this passage from our most devoted servants. Let's be honest—without Martha's tribe, my church would shut down. Outwardly, at least, Martha is a winsome model for the kind of hospitality that Jesus frequently praises and embodies in the gospels. *Outwardly.*

Luke lets us peer through the eyes of Jesus into the chaotic state of Martha's divided heart. For all her hospitality, Martha fails to show a deeper hospitality to the words Jesus wants to speak to her heart. She waits on Jesus, in other words, but she has not time for his words.

Christians have often viewed this passage as a contest between sisters: Mary 1, Martha 0. But what if both messages—the words of commendation to Mary who sits in the posture of a disciple who carefully receives the words of Jesus, and the words of rebuke to Martha—are words of grace? Only in Martha's case, Jesus's words are an invitation for Martha's chaotic heart to finally experience the rest it so richly deserves?

Lord Jesus, speak your peace over our divided hearts right now.

A GIFT, NOT A CHORE
(LUKE 11:1-13)

⁵ Then Jesus said to them, "Suppose you have a friend, and you go to him at midnight and say, 'Friend, lend me three loaves of bread; ⁶ a friend of mine on a journey has come to me, and I have no food to offer him.' ⁷ And suppose the one inside answers, 'Don't bother me. The door is already locked, and my children and I are in bed. I can't get up and give you anything.' ⁸ I tell you, even though he will not get up and give you the bread because of friendship, yet because of your shameless audacity he will surely get up and give you as much as you need."

One of the saddest ironies of the Christian life is that prayer can become a chore we too often postpone (like filing the papers in the bottom of a desk drawer). In reality, prayer is a gift. Is that the secret behind this passage? Is Jesus attempting, in so many different ways, to impress upon his disciples that prayer is not just a solemn responsibility but sheer grace?

If so, perhaps this is why Jesus prays in front of his disciples. It seems to prompt in them a kind of holy envy. When the disciples asked for a primer on prayer to help them keep pace with the disciples of John the

Baptist (v. 1), Jesus over-delivers, giving them a prayer that has centered believers for millennia. His prayer-gift embraces all of life—the mysteries of God and his kingdom, the urgent necessities of daily living, the constant failures which muck up our relationships with God and others, and the fears we have about the evil that lies just around the corner of our lives.

Jesus is still not done. The stories and questions in verses 5-13 practically beg us to pray. There is no inconvenient time to knock on Heaven's door—and there is no good gift a loving Heavenly Father will withhold from you.

> *"Do we want to live without needs? Then we want to live without God. Our needs are a continuous invitation to live in a reality of gift-giving and gift-receiving." (Eugene Peterson,* Tell It Slant*)*

BULLYING THE BULLY
(LUKE 11:14-23)

[14] Jesus was driving out a demon that was mute. When the demon left, the man who had been mute spoke, and the crowd was amazed. [15] But some of them said, "By Beelzebul, the prince of demons, he is driving out demons." [16] Others tested him by asking for a sign from heaven. [17] Jesus knew their thoughts and said to them: "Any kingdom divided against itself will be ruined, and a house divided against itself will fall."

One cold day—one of those empty-church-office days between Christmas and New Years—a ministry colleague and I got a distress call to intervene with barely connected church attenders who were in domestic conflict. While my pastor buddy and I stood on the welcome mat, we could hear the wife's vile screams from a back bedroom. The husband who timidly opened the door was ashen-faced. I began to feel like Evil itself was speaking through these woman's taunts. Everything in me wanted to run.

This memory accompanies my reading of today's passage. Evil and unbelief are palpably present. In one instance, Evil restricts a man from communicating. In another, Evil labels God's holy son a demonic overlord. I want to cry out, *Jesus, run!*

But Jesus does not run. Jesus breaks the conspiracy of silence that keeps a victim from speaking. He exposes the tyranny of lies about his kingdom. He puts the Devil on notice: Christ, the truly Strong Man, has arrived, and he is returning all the Devil's plunder back to its rightful owners. True love, it turns out, is unafraid of bullies.

Jesus, you bind the one who seeks
to keep us captive.

EVIL IN THE ATTIC
(LUKE 11:24-28)

> [24] *"When an impure spirit comes out of a person, it goes through arid places seeking rest and does not find it. Then it says, 'I will return to the house I left.'* [25] *When it arrives, it finds the house swept clean and put in order.* [26] *Then it goes and takes seven other spirits more wicked than itself, and they go in and live there. And the final condition of that person is worse than the first."*

One of the many things I was unprepared for in home ownership was that neighborhood animals might infiltrate our precious domestic space. One spring, a mother raccoon apparently thought our attic would make a nice labor and delivery room for her little kits. While our bedroom ceiling separated us from them, their chaotic noises made it almost impossible for me to sleep. Unfortunately, our adventures at trapping the wily raccoons proved less than successful. We were not at all disappointed when one day they simply disappeared.

Pardon me if I compare that sweet bandit, the raccoon, to the restless demons in this passage, who search relentlessly to find lodging in unsuspecting humans (vv. 24-26). What impresses me most is not Jesus' description of how demons operate (though that is vivid and fascinating) but rather how vulnerable we humans are to powers of evil. Even should we find success in ridding the attic of one varmint, hordes of others are waiting to take its place. We are simply powerless to seal evil out of our lives. What we need rather is the indwelling presence of Christ, who brings us the "word of God" (v. 28).

Jesus, only your presence can fill the vulnerable emptiness of life.

HIDDEN IN PLAIN SIGHT
(LUKE 11:29-36)

> *29 As the crowds increased, Jesus said, "This is a wicked generation. It asks for a sign, but none will be given it except the sign of Jonah. 30 For as Jonah was a sign to the Ninevites, so also will the Son of Man be to this generation."*

It happened again. Next to our kitchen table my wife hung two new 8x11 photos (one of our family and one of our grandbaby), and I did not notice them. They were hidden in plain sight. My eyes managed to miss them as they flitted from phone to plate and back to phone again.

I can't help but see a parallel in the sign-seeking crowds, eyes lighting here and there, looking for some kind of spiritual novelty to entice and distract them. Jesus knows that these are "unhealthy" eyes (v. 34) which allow so little light and faith to enter their shadowy hearts.

All the while, the *true* Sign stands before them, like a practically-drowned-then-resurrected Jonah, seaweed still clinging to his ears, preaching the possibility of rescue to a people seemingly far from redemption. Here stands Jesus, the true Light among them, preaching more wisdom than Solomon could imagine, more hope than anyone can imagine. Here stands Jesus, calling to runaways like Jonah and you and me.

Jesus, direct our distracted eyes toward you.

THE PROBLEM WITH SURFACE READINGS
(LUKE 11:37-54)

37 When Jesus had finished speaking, a Phari-see invited him to eat with him; so he went in and reclined at the table. 38 But the Pharisee was surprised when he noticed that Jesus did not first wash before the meal. 39 Then the Lord said to him, "Now then, you Pharisees clean the outside of the cup and dish, but inside you are full of greed and wickedness. 40 You foolish people! Did not the one who made the outside make the inside also?"

Let's be honest: a surface reading of this text is not flattering toward Jesus. A religious leader invites him for dinner, slightly arches his eyebrows over Jesus' neglecting to engage in ritual hand washing before eating, and Jesus proceeds to go off! He rips into such Pharisees (vv. 39-44), and when one of them tells him that his remarks are hurtful (v. 45), Jesus doubles down for another seven depressing verses! Backed into a corner, it seems only natural that the Pharisees would "oppose him fiercely" (v. 53).

The problem, of course, is with "surface" readings. Showy religion concentrates on the "surfaces" of things, shiny and pious exteriors that conceal an inner greed and pretense and even dangerous heartlessness toward the people we say we love.

As a member of a professional religious class of people, I too am stung that Jesus is saying these things out loud. I know that I am more motivated to polish the impression I make upon church members than to attend to the state of my soul. It is highly offensive precisely because it rings true. And I can either give into a craven animosity toward Jesus (the whistleblower on the inner debris in my soul), or I can drop to my knees before him and cry out: "Do something!"

Jesus, clean all of it.

LEARNING WHAT TO FEAR
(LUKE 12:1-12)

⁴ "I tell you, my friends, do not be afraid of those who kill the body and after that can do no more. ⁵ But I will show you whom you should fear: Fear him who, after your body has been killed, has authority to throw you into hell. Yes, I tell you, fear him. ⁶ Are not five sparrows sold for two pennies? Yet not one of them is forgotten by God. ⁷ Indeed, the very hairs of your head are all numbered. Don't be afraid; you are worth more than many sparrows.

One of the earliest rhymes I learned—"Red and yellow kill a fellow; red and black, venom lack"—has a useful purpose behind it. Coral snakes, with their red and yellow touching, are venomous. Scarlet king snakes, with red and black touching, are harmless. These two snakes closely resemble one another, but discerning eyes tell us which one to fear.

One of the persistent dangers in the Christian life is that we play with situations that can harm us and run from those the Holy Spirit has ordained for us. For example, Jesus warns us against the "yeast" of hypocrisy and hiding our sin (vv. 1-2). He warns against ignoring and denying God. Like the coral snake, these temptations can seriously harm us. The people the disciples (rightly) feared held immense power in this life. Still, they cannot ultimately harm our relationship with God (vv. 6-7). Even when the world wounds, the Holy Spirit's presence never leaves us (vv. 11-12)

Warning and reassurance—these are not contradictions, but lessons in discernment, instructing me always to turn toward the one whose *eye is on the sparrow.*

"Teach us to care and not to care"
(T.S. Eliot, "Ash Wednesday")

PRAYING TO MYSELF
(LUKE 12:13-31)

¹⁶ And he told them this parable: "The ground of a certain rich man yielded an abundant harvest. ¹⁷ He thought to himself, 'What shall I do? I have no place to store my crops.' ¹⁸ Then he said, 'This is what I'll do. I will tear down my barns and build bigger ones, and there I will store my surplus grain. ¹⁹ And I'll say to myself, 'You have plenty of grain laid up for many years. Take life easy; eat, drink and be merry.' ²⁰ But God said to him, 'You fool! This very night your life will be demanded from you. Then who will get what you have prepared for yourself?' ²¹ This is how it will be with whoever stores up things for themselves but is not rich toward God."

Two things unnerve me about Jesus' "bigger barns" parable. The first is the seductive fantasy which undergirds the story. Who doesn't secretly long for an unanticipated "bumper crop," the agricultural equivalent of striking oil or winning the lottery? I struggle with how much that "eat, drink, and be merry" lifestyle appeals to me.

The second concern is deeper. This farmer's actions have a certain earthly logic to them. We do not stop to consider why we are blessed, nor do we utter a prayer as to how we should respond. We spend time and money to spend more time making money. Instead of asking God how to respond to life's unexpected blessings, self-talk swallows prayer—there is only "I" and "my" and "myself." And where does all this lead? To a misplaced vision of "heaven on earth," as if we are guaranteed an earthly eternity on which to gorge ourselves.

May God rescue us from such sinister logic before death does the job (v. 20). May God convince us, deep down, that our true life can never be equated with "an abundance of possessions" (v. 15).

Jesus, save us from ourselves.

DECONSTRUCTING WORRY
(LUKE 12:22-34)

> [22] *Then Jesus said to his disciples: "Therefore I tell you, do not worry about your life, what you will eat; or about your body, what you will wear.* [23] *For life is more than food, and the body more than clothes.* [24] *Consider the ravens: They do not sow or reap, they have no storeroom or barn; yet God feeds them. And how much more valuable you are than birds!* [25] *Who of you by worrying can add a single hour to your life?"*

Three words in verse 22 almost have an air of fantasy about them, comparable to "climb Everest" or "stop blinking." They are: "do not worry." And yet, as I keep reading, I can't disagree with the points Jesus is making. I know that worry narrows my life (v. 23), that it is inconsistent with my belief in a loving and trustworthy God (v. 24), and that it is a worthless strategy for living (not only will it not "add a single hour to your life," it will likely subtract many hours from our lives!).

Still, even as I write these words on a lovely morning in May, my mind is distracted by a home repair that I fear will be costly. I know that if I am to experience peace in the midst of life's worries, it will not come from my willpower. It will only happen as Jesus' words overpower with my heart, less as a demand and more as an embrace. As if Jesus is saying, "You let me worry about these things for a while. And while I do, spend a little time 'worrying' about my Kingdom and your investment in it." How kind of Jesus to flood my life with his generous care and to use personal generosity to take my mind off my fears.

> *"Do not be afraid, little flock, for your Father has been pleased to give you the kingdom."*
> *(Luke 12:32)*

I'M AWAKE?
(LUKE 12:35-48)

³⁵ "Be dressed ready for service and keep your lamps burning, ³⁶ like servants waiting for their master to return from a wedding banquet, so that when he comes and knocks they can immediately open the door for him. ³⁷ It will be good for those servants whose master finds them watching when he comes. Truly I tell you, he will dress himself to serve, will have them recline at the table and will come and wait on them. ³⁸ It will be good for those servants whose master finds them ready, even if he comes in the middle of the night or toward daybreak."

It was time for the two of us to lead a mid-morning session at a college retreat, he the singer and me the preacher. I knocked on his cabin door, and after no response, I knocked again. Finally, he opened the door, his long hair extremely lopsided, and the first thing he said was, "I'm awake." *Sure you are.*

Jesus frequently uses the image of the unexpected knock on the door when the master returns. In today's readings, ready servants *expect* the knock, while wicked servants abuse the master's people and wine cellar as if the master will never return (v. 45).

As much as I'd rather not lump myself in with the wicked servants, I know I can live senseless of the master—out of sight, out of mind. My only prayer is for a gift of faith in a grace that never sleeps, and that such faith will turn to joy when the master returns to "dress himself to serve" me, of all people (v. 37).

Jesus, thank you for the gift of faith that hears
the knock and opens the door.

A DIFFERENT TYPE OF FORECASTING
(LUKE 12:49-59)

[54] He said to the crowd: "When you see a cloud rising in the west, immediately you say, 'It's going to rain,' and it does. [55] And when the south wind blows, you say, 'It's going to be hot,' and it is. [56] Hypocrites! You know how to interpret the appearance of the earth and the sky. How is it that you don't know how to interpret this present time?"

I have a certain amount of compassion for meteorologists. How would you like to be the one who predicts sunshine on Labor Day, only to see people's picnics rained out? I have even heard of a poor weatherman whom some viewers have dubbed "Dead Wrong Dennis" because of his frequent misinterpretations of nature's mysterious movements.

In the heart of today's passage, Jesus calls out some forecasters who pride themselves on prophesying rainy skies and scorching winds yet cannot read the signs of the times (v. 56). They are already missing out on the biggest cosmic disturbance ever—the visitation of Jesus to our planet. Jesus says that he will undergo a deluge of suffering on the cross (v. 50), a sign of his fiery judgment on sin and evil powers (v. 49). Intimate family members will divide over this sign-to-end-all-signs (vv. 51-53).

And the wise among us? We will not be lulled by the fair-weather promises of a culturally comfortable peace. No, we will throw ourselves at the feet of this Savior and Judge and plead for the mercy that only he can provide.

Jesus, we praise you for a forecast of undeserved mercy.

A MOMENTARY STAY
OF EXECUTION
(LUKE 13:1-9)

⁶ Then he told this parable: "A man had a fig tree growing in his vineyard, and he went to look for fruit on it but did not find any. ⁷ So he said to the man who took care of the vineyard, 'For three years now I've been coming to look for fruit on this fig tree and haven't found any. Cut it down! Why should it use up the soil?' ⁸ 'Sir,' the man replied, 'leave it alone for one more year, and I'll dig around it and fertilize it. ⁹ If it bears fruit next year, fine! If not, then cut it down.'"

The Jesus we find in these verses would have received low marks in my seminary's "Pastoral Care" class. Some people in the crowd approach Jesus with news of a violent tragedy—Pilate has murdered Galileans, their blood mixing with the sacrifices they brought to the Temple. If the people were looking to Pastor Jesus in that moment to do some handholding, or censure of Rome's cruelty, or offer assurances that God would never let an evil outcome like that fall on their righteous heads, Jesus does not give it to them. He piles on instead, mentioning a catastrophic collapse of a tower in Jerusalem, and noting that the victims were no less sinful than those Jesus was staring at in this present moment.

There is no vaccine that inoculates us from evil people and tragic circumstances. There is only this moment and, we pray, the next moment and a next after that. Is that bad news or good news? It depends. The fruitless fig tree in Jesus' parable does not have all of eternity to waste the farmer's time (vv. 6-9). Still, there is this moment, a stay of execution, a window for Christ's grace to produce improbable fruit.

Jesus, help us bear fruit.

TOES TO NOSE
(LUKE 13:10-21)

¹⁰ On a Sabbath Jesus was teaching in one of the synagogues, ¹¹ and a woman was there who had been crippled by a spirit for eighteen years. She was bent over and could not straighten up at all. ¹² When Jesus saw her, he called her forward and said to her, "Woman, you are set free from your infirmity." ¹³ Then he put his hands on her, and immediately she straightened up and praised God.

As often happens in the gospels, two stories intersect in one space and time—in this case, a synagogue on a Sabbath day. One is a story of *theological* conflict. A synagogue leader and his friends, viewing the Sabbath primarily through the eyes of restriction, claim that these people who seek a miracle are requesting a "work" that is forbidden. Jesus instead sees the Sabbath as an opportunity for grace, and even his opponents hypocritically show such grace to their farm animals (v. 15).

The other is a *spiritual* conflict. A woman, "crippled" by an evil spirit and who has consequently been physically bent over for eighteen years, is now liberated from her bondage. She walked in seeing only Jesus' toes, but she will now praise him to his face.

The reign of Jesus may at times appear small and weak, like tiny seeds or hidden yeast. Don't underestimate him. He rescues you as much from distorted religion as he does the powers of evil that keep you bent inward against yourself—even if it takes eighteen years, or more.

Jesus, raise my eyes to behold your
healing face.

FROM THEORETICAL
TO PERSONAL
(LUKE 13:22-30)

²³ Someone asked him, "Lord, are only a few people going to be saved?" He said to them, ²⁴ "Make every effort to enter through the narrow door, because many, I tell you, will try to enter and will not be able to. ²⁵ Once the owner of the house gets up and closes the door, you will stand outside knocking and pleading, 'Sir, open the door for us.' "But he will answer, 'I don't know you or where you come from.'"

Jesus responds to a *theoretical* question (about the number of people who will be saved) with a *personal* challenge (about a "narrow door" which is currently opened but will one day shut). I will be honest—I don't enjoy it when Jesus talks like this. It depresses me to think about people shut out from God's heavenly banquet (v. 29), and it is frightening to imagine for a moment Jesus telling me that he doesn't know me after all the time I've spent professing to know him (vv. 26-27).

I don't *like* that kind of talk, but I *need* it. I need to avoid the high and narrow perch of those religious people who look down their long noses at those people who appear to come in "last" in any religious contest. I need to remember that Jesus is unimpressed with my religious resume. I need to think about that "narrow door" to salvation—about as narrow as Jesus' outstretched arms on the cross. I need to thank God for grace that secures a seat at the banquet which my life could never finance. I need all of it.

Jesus, to open up the door to heaven, you became last for us (v. 30).

FINISHING THE JOB
(LUKE 13:31-35)

> *31 At that time some Pharisees came to Jesus and said to him, "Leave this place and go somewhere else. Herod wants to kill you." 32 He replied, "Go tell that fox, 'I will keep on driving out demons and healing people today and tomorrow, and on the third day I will reach my goal.' 33 In any case, I must press on today and tomorrow and the next day—for surely no prophet can die outside Jerusalem!"*

One Saturday I asked my teenage boys to rake a massive amount of fall leaves that were piling up in our backyard. By nightfall, the leaves were mostly spread around into piles, but few ended up in bags. So on Monday morning I announced to them that I would pay two dollars for every *bag* of leaves. When I pulled into the driveway that evening there were thirty bags out by our fence. Something had changed.

Jesus possessed an otherworldly motivation to finish his work of redemption. He would not be rushed, nor would he be dissuaded by the rumors of religious leaders or the threat of political leaders (v. 31). Jerusalem's dismal record for treating unpopular prophets would not deter him (v. 34). Jesus refused to turn his back on children, who like rebellious "chicks," had fled the safety of mother's wings (v. 34). He would finish the job of redemption on the cross and rise again on the "third day" (v. 32). Jesus said he would finish the job, and by God, he meant it.

Jesus, by your grace gather us redeemed rebels
to your side again.

A RELIGION IN NEED
OF HEALING
(LUKE 14:1-6)

³ Jesus asked the Pharisees and experts in the law, "Is it lawful to heal on the Sabbath or not?" ⁴ But they remained silent. So taking hold of the man, he healed him and sent him on his way. ⁵ Then he asked them, "If one of you has a child or an ox that falls into a well on the Sabbath day, will you not immediately pull it out?" ⁶ And they had nothing to say.

An eerie silence hovers over this passage like fog. Jesus, the guest of a leading Pharisee, can feel the wordless scrutiny of the theological crowd with whom he dines. Their eyes are darting back and forth between Jesus and the sick man who has suddenly entered the dining room. On this Sabbath day, they wonder if Jesus will break their laws by doing a "work" of healing—and Jesus does just that (v. 4).

That healing, however, takes a back seat to the one-sided dialogue Jesus has with his critics. He first wants to put them on record about whether they truly believe that "healing" and "Sabbath" have irreconcilable differences. But he deepens that first question with a follow up. *So you're telling me that if your son—no, not even your son, let's say your ox—falls down in a hole on the Sabbath, you're just going to let them lie there all day?* Both times, Jesus' opponents fall silent. I mean, what do you say, when even you find your own religion deficient in the love your religion calls you to pursue?

Jesus, heal our sick theology too.

DOWNWARDLY MOBILE
(LUKE 14:7-14)

[8] *"When someone invites you to a wedding feast, do not take the place of honor, for a person more distinguished than you may have been invited. [9] If so, the host who invited both of you will come and say to you, 'Give this person your seat.' Then, humiliated, you will have to take the least important place. [10] But when you are invited, take the lowest place, so that when your host comes, he will say to you, 'Friend, move up to a better place.' Then you will be honored in the presence of all the other guests. [11] For all those who exalt themselves will be humbled, and those who humble themselves will be exalted."*

Here Jesus has our social ambitions in view. He highlights this tendency we have to position ourselves near the best people in the best places. How humiliating it is when our social striving backfires, when we end up at the nerd table rather than the cool table we initially sought. The force of the law is painful: "all those who exalt themselves will be humbled" (v. 11), indeed, "humiliated" (v. 9).

But grace is displayed vividly as well, in the party one throws not for the upwardly mobile but the downwardly mired (e.g., "the poor, the crippled, the lame, the blind"). Such generosity, given for generosity's sake, brings its own joy. This is grace: someone gives (technically, "imputes") something another does not deserve, and joy redounds to all associated with the giving.

Jesus, you invite us least deserving to the best banquet of all.

HEARTBREAK AND
HOPEFULNESS
(LUKE 14:15-24)

¹⁵ When one of those at the table with him heard this, he said to Jesus, "Blessed is the one who will eat at the feast in the kingdom of God." ¹⁶ Jesus replied: "A certain man was preparing a great banquet and invited many guests. ¹⁷ At the time of the banquet he sent his servant to tell those who had been invited, 'Come, for everything is now ready.' ¹⁸ But they all alike began to make excuses. The first said, 'I have just bought a field, and I must go and see it. Please excuse me.'"

Religion at its worst takes on a note of smug self-congratulation. That's how I read the comment from Jesus' dinner guest—"Blessed is the one who will eat at the feast in the kingdom of God" (v. 15). As if the man is saying to his co-religionists, "It is good to be us, the happy few, the righteous!"

Perhaps that is why Jesus tells this story, with all the heartbreak and hopefulness of our Christian life together. While Jesus' dinner guests are celebrating their future experience of the kingdom of God in heaven, Jesus wants them to know that the kingdom of God is already here, in him. He lays it out in the image of an invitation to a sumptuous banquet (one to which, in actuality, Jesus is both the host and the courier). Unfortunately, many who are invited to dine on Jesus' gospel demonstrate that they have better things to do (vv. 18-20). There is the heartbreak—the refusal of the host's invitation is no trivial matter.

For me, however, the heartbreak is overcome by the hopefulness of those who recognize the good news in this invitation. Indeed, the following words drip with grace:

- *"Come."*
- *"Everything is now ready."*
- *"Great banquet."*
- *"There is still room."*
- *"My house will be full."*

Jesus, blessed are the unworthy who somehow find their name cards on your Father's table.

THE GOSPEL IS NOT
A SIDE DISH
(LUKE 14:25-35)

25 Large crowds were traveling with Jesus, and turning to them he said: 26 "If anyone comes to me and does not hate father and mother, wife and children, brothers and sisters—yes, even their own life—such a person cannot be my disciple. 27 And whoever does not carry their cross and follow me cannot be my disciple. 28 Suppose one of you wants to build a tower. Won't you first sit down and estimate the cost to see if you have enough money to complete it?"

During my Christian adolescence, I heard the reading of an essay at a church gathering that has never left me: "I would like to buy $3 worth of God please. Not enough to explode my soul or disturb my sleep, but just enough to equal a cup of warm milk or a snooze in the sunshine."[3] I still find these words to be a helpful platform from which to view the stark words and parables in today's reading.

Jesus is not offering us $3 worth of religious inspiration here, something we can mix and match with other contemporary spiritualities. The gospel inevitably divides—as easily as it draws some it alienates others

(v. 26). If you give mere lip service to the gospel, you will only succeed in looking foolish, like an abandoned, half-built tower or, worse, like an out-matched army (vv. 28-32). At the center of the gospel is a cross (v. 27), and the cross is death, a death that necessarily precedes Christ's resurrection and ours.[4] But if this world has proved anything to us, death comes regardless. Why not let Christ's death be our starting point, and find our true lives on the other side of it?

> *"For you died, and your life is now hidden*
> *with Christ in God." (Colossians 3:3)*

AGAINST MY BETTER
JUDGMENT
(LUKE 15:1-10)

> *⁴ "Suppose one of you has a hundred sheep and loses one of them. Doesn't he leave the ninety-nine in the open country and go after the lost sheep until he finds it? ⁵ And when he finds it, he joyfully puts it on his shoulders ⁶ and goes home. Then he calls his friends and neighbors together and says, 'Rejoice with me; I have found my lost sheep.'"*

"I say we should cut our losses." That's a statement I frequently hear when discussing the business of the church. In fact, I am quite grateful for business-minded lay leaders who help me make tough and prudent decisions about profit and loss. Still, I must conclude from today's passage that the priorities of Jesus don't always add up.

Instead of "cut our losses," I hear a different phrase: "against my better judgment." That's what we say, don't we, when we find ourselves on a risky and time-consuming mission? For the foolish shepherd who risks the safety of the well-behaved ninety-nine to go after the rebellious one? Who brings the derelict sheep home on his shoulders, as if this rogue sheep is, in fact, some

lost prince? Has he lost all sense of judgment and pro-
priety?

Against his better judgment, Jesus will not stop
searching for bad investments. Against his better judgment, he will not stop celebrating their return. Against
his better judgment, he will not cut his losses with
these disreputable "tax collectors and sinners" who keep
demanding his attention (v. 1). Against his better judgment, Jesus will not stop.

Jesus, I take comfort in your relentless search
for lost causes.

THEOLOGY IN MINIATURE
(LUKE 15:11-32)

[31] "'My son,' the father said, 'you are always with me, and everything I have is yours. [32] But we had to celebrate and be glad, because this brother of yours was dead and is alive again; he was lost and is found.'"

Imagine for a moment that Christians carry around a truncated Bible in their heads. In this mental Bible are all the verses, stories, and images from Scripture which have made the deepest imprint on us. For so many years, this story of a father's love for his wayward younger son has resided in the deepest core of my theology. I see the life of faith through its word-pictures: our senseless rebellion against our generous father, the feckless friends and wasted days of sinful living, the spiritual sobriety that begins to emerge when we "come to our senses," and the wholly undignified running of the father to welcome back his undeserving children. This parable glues all my theology together.

Still, for so many years, I held an abridged view of this parable in my mind. It was for me, all about the younger son who sinned in dramatic, tabloid fashion in Sin City. His older brother, the "good" one, was relegated to the background. It took an unnecessarily long time for me to recognize that his story is also my own.

Sly sinners like the elder brother conceal a seething self-righteousness and absurd resentment and can be "lost" while never venturing all that far from home.

And yet the Father pursues both of us to welcome us back home.

Jesus, your grace brings dead prodigals back to life again (v. 32).

BLESSED ARE THE SHREWD
(LUKE 16:1-13)

> [8] *"The master commended the dishonest manager because he had acted shrewdly. For the people of this world are more shrewd in dealing with their own kind than are the people of the light.* [9] *I tell you, use worldly wealth to gain friends for yourselves, so that when it is gone, you will be welcomed into eternal dwellings."*

Okay, wait, what? A manager has been skimming off his rich boss. The boss finds out and demands a final accounting before his termination is complete. In the meantime, the manager goes out to make fast friends by lowering the debts owed to the boss. And here's the kicker: when the boss finds out, he praises the dishonest manager! No wonder that if there is any consensus about this parable, it is that it is the most difficult to interpret. So if you are expecting me to finally solve the puzzle that has stymied so many wise commentators, I am sorry to disappoint you.

Still, maybe just one little thought before I go. The dishonest manager comes to the dead-end of life as he has known it—in this case, a life in service to a master called "Money" (v. 13). His self-talk is filled with weakness and fear (v. 3)—he lacks all the resources he needs to climb out of this hole he has dug for himself. He has made a mess of his past, and his only hope is ingratiating himself to friends who can secure his future.

What this man needs, more than Money, is a *friend*. How *shrewd* to cut our losses and to throw ourselves at the mercy of the one who calls Himself our "friend" (John 15:15).

Jesus, give us a holy shrewdness about which
Master can truly save us.

TRYING TO FOOL THE SCALE
(LUKE 16:14-18)

14 The Pharisees, who loved money, heard all this and were sneering at Jesus. 15 He said to them, "You are the ones who justify yourselves in the eyes of others, but God knows your hearts. What people value highly is detestable in God's sight. 16 The Law and the Prophets were proclaimed until John. Since that time, the good news of the kingdom of God is being preached, and everyone is forcing their way into it. 17 It is easier for heaven and earth to disappear than for the least stroke of a pen to drop out of the Law."

Whenever I go to the doctor's office, they rudely request that I step on the scale. Sometimes I slip off my shoes and jacket, take my smartphone and keys out of my pocket, and hold my breath before I step up. Still, the reading is pitiless. It dares to pronounce a number five pounds higher than the last time I stepped on it. It makes a mockery of my professed commitment to a healthy lifestyle.

In today's reading, the Law is just as pitiless. The Pharisees, who have arranged their exterior lives to give the appearance of being law-abiding, cannot hide their insides from the God who "knows [their] hearts" (v. 15).

Contrary to their claims, Jesus is not anti-Law (v. 17). In fact, Jesus fully upholds the laws that some of his opponents would like to shirk, impressing upon them God's expectations concerning our greed (v. 14) and our lax commitment to marital fidelity (v. 18).

The scale of the Law is not our friend, and our attempts to justify ourselves (v. 15) will always fail. Our one hope, our *only* hope, is sunk deep in "the good news of the kingdom of God" (v. 16) which Jesus came to preach—and to enact on behalf of our law-breaking souls.

Jesus, you weigh us on scales of mercy.

GOOD NEWS EMBEDDED
IN A NIGHTMARE
(LUKE 16:19-31)

[19] "There was a rich man who was dressed in purple and fine linen and lived in luxury every day. [20] At his gate was laid a beggar named Lazarus, covered with sores [21] and longing to eat what fell from the rich man's table. Even the dogs came and licked his sores. [22] The time came when the beggar died and the angels carried him to Abraham's side. The rich man also died and was buried."

You might not want to read this passage too close to bedtime—it is a living nightmare, at least for the rich man. He has stuffed his earthly days full of a materialist's heaven, living in "luxury every day" (v. 19). On earth, he will not be moved by the brevity of time, the pain of the poor (v. 20), the warnings of Scripture (v. 29), nor presumably even the testimony of resurrection (v. 31). In a chapter about the dangers of wealth, this parable provides a fitting and frightening conclusion. If it alerts us to the dangers of greed long enough to see the invisible poor nearby, that will be a good thing for both rich and poor.

Yet there is more than nightmare here. If we see Lazarus as the Christ-figure (as Robert Capon advises [5]), then we will not only embrace the inevitability of death but also trust that Jesus overcomes death. We will find ourselves hidden in the suffering death of our Lazarus, and against all odds, rise to new life in Him.

> *"All those the Father gives me will come to me, and whoever comes to me I will never drive away." (John 6:37)*

ATTENTION!
(LUKE 17:1-10)

[7] "Suppose one of you has a servant plowing or looking after the sheep. Will he say to the servant when he comes in from the field, 'Come along now and sit down to eat'? [8] Won't he rather say, 'Prepare my supper, get yourself ready and wait on me while I eat and drink; after that you may eat and drink'? [9] Will he thank the servant because he did what he was told to do? [10] So you also, when you have done everything you were told to do, should say, 'We are unworthy servants; we have only done our duty.'"

My dad once described for me the jarring sensation of his first days at Army boot camp. He wasn't used to being yelled at, woken up in the middle of the night, or having to pay so much attention to the way his bed was made or his shoes were shined. "They were trying to train me to think in a whole new way regarding authority," he said.

Now, if you conclude I'm comparing Jesus in today's text to a drill sergeant, my illustration has obviously failed. Still, as Jesus spent much of Chapter 16 exposing the flawed thinking of religious leaders, his bracing words also expose our unredeemed inner lives. Jesus' words lead us to new perspectives about protecting the vulnerable (vv. 1-2), living graciously with those who fail us (vv. 3-4), and seeing ourselves as servants rather than those impatient to be served (vv. 7-10).

I can't imagine a better response to such hard words than the cry of the apostles: "Increase our faith! (v. 5)." Thankfully, this is a prayer our gracious Savior loves to answer.

Jesus, increase our faith!

THE REAL HERO
(LUKE 17:11-19)

[15] One of them, when he saw he was healed, came back, praising God in a loud voice. [16] He threw himself at Jesus' feet and thanked him— and he was a Samaritan. [17] Jesus asked, "Were not all ten cleansed? Where are the other nine? [18] Has no one returned to give praise to God except this foreigner?" [19] Then he said to him, "Rise and go; your faith has made you well."

Early in my life, pious Sunday School teachers shamed me for being a Ninety-Percenter, a boy who was only after what he could get from Jesus, too lazy to retrace his steps to give Jesus a proper thank you. Likewise, teachers elevated this tenth man, a Samaritan leper, a double-outsider among polite Jewish society. To be sure, his gratitude is impressive, as he walks far and praises loudly and prostrates himself vigorously at the feet of Jesus.

In my memories of countless sermons and children's story times on this passage, Jesus rarely gets top billing. The tenth leper was always in the spotlight. Yet why was Jesus traveling to border towns (v. 11) and hanging out with the physically contagious and, in the case of the Samaritan, the religiously suspect (v. 1)? How is it that Jesus finds Himself irresistibly drawn to our pleas for mercy (v. 13)? Why does Jesus choose in this moment to exalt the Samaritan over himself? Why does he pronounce a second miracle, a "wellness" that goes much deeper than his diseased skin (v. 19)?

I've got nothing against the tenth leper. I truly crave more of his faith, his gratitude, and his unembarrassed ardor. But Jesus is the hero here—here and always.

"Jesus, Master, have pity on us!" (v.13).

THE SPEED OF LOVE
(LUKE 17:20-37)

[20] Once, on being asked by the Pharisees when the kingdom of God would come, Jesus replied, "The coming of the kingdom of God is not something that can be observed, [21] nor will people say, 'Here it is,' or 'There it is,' because the kingdom of God is in your midst." [22] Then he said to his disciples, "The time is coming when you will long to see one of the days of the Son of Man, but you will not see it. [23] People will tell you, 'There he is!' or 'Here he is!' Do not go running off after them."

The theologian Kosuke Koyama wrote a book with a beautiful title: *Three Mile an Hour God.* The book claims that God, who is love, chooses to walk slowly, to walk the speed we walk, to show love to us. This, Koyama says, is the "speed of love." This is the speed at which Jesus walks throughout the gospel of Luke, pausing, digressing, serving up new teaching and healing to reveal that God's Kingdom is now "in your midst."

It is not only religious sophisticates (v. 20) who lack patience for strolling with Jesus. So many of us want to race toward the cataclysmic "signs" that validate our faith (yet negotiate daily life on our own). The problem with signs is that we often mistake them (v. 23), and when God's judgment falls "like lightning," it is too late to prepare for it (vv. 26-27). Even those who are given the grace of warning and space for repentance often, like Lot's wife (v. 32), turn our faces away from an escape and try to save an old life not worth rescuing (v. 33).

The words of this passage are frightening for those who care more about manipulating signs than spending time with the Savior. But still Jesus walks, three miles an hour, sharing His kingdom in our midst.

Jesus, let your daily grace be "sign" enough for me.

DON'T GIVE UP
(LUKE 18:1-8)

[4] *"For some time he refused. But finally he said to himself, 'Even though I don't fear God or care what people think, [5] yet because this widow keeps bothering me, I will see that she gets justice, so that she won't eventually come and attack me!'" [6] And the Lord said, "Listen to what the unjust judge says. [7] And will not God bring about justice for his chosen ones, who cry out to him day and night? Will he keep putting them off? [8] I tell you, he will see that they get justice, and quickly. However, when the Son of Man comes, will he find faith on the earth?"*

Perhaps you've taken that literature class where you are assigned a novel or short story to interpret. You scour the characters and plot and images, nervously searching for "the theme." In this parable, Luke saves us from all that work, telling us upfront that in telling this story Jesus' purpose for his listeners is that "they should always pray and not give up" (v. 1).

Still, the story is strange, heartbreaking, and comic, simultaneously. A spectacularly unprincipled judge is constantly harangued by a victimized widow. In the end, the judge reveals the moral and spiritual vacuum in his own heart yet still rules in favor of the widow, completely for self-serving reasons. The judge has been worn down by the frequent court appearances of the widow, even to the point of fearing for his life!

Like so many of Jesus' teachings, the throughline travels from *lesser to the greater*. If even a corrupt judge eventually listens to a widow's plea, how will a loving God respond to our prayers? "Will he keep putting them off" (v. 7)? Faith's answer is a defiant "no."

By the time we arrive at the parable's end, the characters have reversed. God comes to us like a persistent widow, begging us to place our miniscule faith in him and pray.

Jesus, plant a faith in us that outlasts the long delays of justice.

"GOD HAVE MERCY!"
(LUKE 18:9-14)

[13] "But the tax collector stood at a distance. He would not even look up to heaven, but beat his breast and said, 'God, have mercy on me, a sinner.' [14] I tell you that this man, rather than the other, went home justified before God. For all those who exalt themselves will be humbled, and those who humble themselves will be exalted."

What a gift this passage is! In the first place, it runs a journalistic exposé on the corrupt core of self-righteous religion. That person long held up as an exemplar to young and aspiring religionists? That respectable churchman who scrupulously tithes and greatly distances himself from the worst kind of people? He's a phony! His ultimate trust is in himself, not God (v. 9). His prayer is more self-congratulation than an honest entreaty to God. His concern is with the moral distance between himself and other sinners, not the chasm which separates him from God. For the moment, I exult in the fact that this religious jerk will get what's coming to him (v. 14); that moment is up when I realize that jerk is me!

Thankfully, there is a second and more hopeful message in this parable. This tax collector who has sold out his own people has nothing to bring to God, and he knows it. His sin is so heavy on him that he can't even risk eye contact with God. How can it be that the prayer that emerges from his notorious lips has morphed into one of the most significant in Christian history—the famed "Jesus Prayer"—"God be merciful to me, a sinner" (v. 13)? What a gift: justification for those like me who least deserve it!

Lord Jesus Christ, son of God, have mercy on me, a sinner.

THE OPPOSITE OF SOCIAL CLIMBING (LUKE 18:15-17)

¹⁵ People were also bringing babies to Jesus for him to place his hands on them. When the disciples saw this, they rebuked them. ¹⁶ But Jesus called the children to him and said, "Let the little children come to me, and do not hinder them, for the kingdom of God belongs to such as these. ¹⁷ Truly I tell you, anyone who will not receive the kingdom of God like a little child will never enter it."

Picture yourself at an A-level social event. A few people in the room could advance your job prospects or social standing, while most could not. As often happens, the first people to greet you are on the less-expedient side of the room. As you embrace them, you can't help surreptitiously looking over their shoulders, plotting how you can quickly disentangle yourselves from this conversation to introduce yourself to those who might be advantageous to you.

Cynical? Yes, and yet this kind of social climbing was typical even in Jesus' day. At that time, children were considered the least significant (especially "babies"—v. 15). The disciples tried to protect their popular leader from taxing interactions that were, from their point of view, a waste of time. They rebuke these annoying parents, but Jesus quickly overrules them and welcomes the children.

Jesus does something else at the same time: He flouts society's scales of useful-to-useless. He looks over the shoulders of the self-important toward those who have nothing to offer Him. He ensures that these are touched, welcomed, blessed.

Jesus, you bless even me.

THE IMPOSSIBLE POSSIBILITY
(LUKE 18:18-34)

> *[24] Jesus looked at him and said, "How hard it is for the rich to enter the kingdom of God! [25] Indeed, it is easier for a camel to go through the eye of a needle than for someone who is rich to enter the kingdom of God." [26] Those who heard this asked, "Who then can be saved?" [27] Jesus replied, "What is impossible with man is possible with God."*

Reader beware: these are hard words. I find an unfortunate resonance with that "certain ruler." Like him, I strive to keep the Ten Commandments, and I have a deep and hidden attachment to my possessions. Putting myself in that man's sandals, I am horrified to hear Jesus say that the "one thing" I lack is the one thing I too often cling to—my earthly security blanket, my standard of living, my stuff. I am like that camel trying to thread the needle of God's holiness. I need to hear how often my stuff keeps me from honoring the First Commandment to have "no other gods before me" but our good God. I need God to scan my heart.

I also desperately need the second half of this passage (vv. 26-30). When the disciples hear the devastating demands of Jesus and cry out—"Who then can be saved?"—Jesus sounds the grace note I can't live without. If salvation is measured by our obedience, it is impossible. Yet, Jesus says in verse 27, "What is impossible with man is possible with God." This verse is my life raft, tossed out toward my flailing arms.

Jesus, your grace makes the impossible possible.

THE SHOUT ABOVE THE SHOUT
(LUKE 18:35-43)

> *39 Those who led the way rebuked him and told him to be quiet, but he shouted all the more, "Son of David, have mercy on me!" 40 Jesus stopped and ordered the man to be brought to him. When he came near, Jesus asked him, 41 "What do you want me to do for you?" "Lord, I want to see," he replied.*

At a conference on spiritual direction, the facilitator seized on that question Jesus asks in verse 41: "What do you want me to do for you?" How rarely we associate that question with the traditional Christianity. We expect a holy God to make mincemeat of our desires. *Your desires are the problem,* we've been told over and over.

The blind beggar must have heard it, too: "Your desire is out of bounds—be quiet." Still, he shouts out, and when Jericho parade-watchers try to shout him down, he shouts over them (v. 39). In my imagination, the word that rises highest above the din is that one word, "mercy!" (v. 39). That word "mercy" was most often heard as a cry for alms to replace the wages he could never earn.

Oddly, Jesus wants us voice the desires at the core of our hearts.

Jesus, we want to see.

AN INEXPLICABLE COMPULSION
(LUKE 19:1-10)

> *3 He wanted to see who Jesus was, but because he was short he could not see over the crowd. 4 So he ran ahead and climbed a sycamore-fig tree to see him, since Jesus was coming that way. 5 When Jesus reached the spot, he looked up and said to him, "Zacchaeus, come down immediately. I must stay at your house today." 6 So he came down at once and welcomed him gladly.*

When a local pariah named Zacchaeus set out for a look at the Jesus parade (v. 3), that was likely all he could reasonably hope for—a glimpse at Jesus. Perhaps, as this short man peered through large sycamore leaves, it was a *guilty* look, one conscious of greed and fraud. Could Zacchaeus have even dreamed when he woke that morning of what his eyes would see and ears would hear?

One word he heard Jesus speak, in the original language, has a sense of divine compulsion about it: "I must stay at your house today" (v. 5). The idea behind the Greek verb communicates this tone: "Look, Zacchaeus, you're not going to believe this, but I absolutely have to have lunch with you in your home today. God has decided it; resistance is futile!"

God must have decided it because nothing else makes sense. Zacchaeus does not deserve an audience with Jesus—he knows it, and so do all the bitter townspeople of Jericho (v. 7), who had tried to box him out. Nothing could ever explain the sheer grace that sought Zacchaeus and brought salvation to his home (v. 10), this grace that also prompted the fresh fruit of repentance (v. 8). If you can find a logical explanation for Jesus' divine compulsion to enter your life, it is not grace.

Jesus, "I must stay at your house today."

THAT BLASTED NAPKIN
(LUKE 19:11-27)

²⁰ "Then another servant came and said, 'Sir, here is your mina; I have kept it laid away in a piece of cloth. ²¹ I was afraid of you, because you are a hard man. You take out what you did not put in and reap what you did not sow.' ²² His master replied, 'I will judge you by your own words, you wicked servant! You knew, did you, that I am a hard man, taking out what I did not put in, and reaping what I did not sow? ²³ Why then didn't you put my money on deposit, so that when I came back, I could have collected it with interest?'"

Family members of mine told me a story about getting the house of a dearly departed loved one ready for sale. As they were cleaning and packing, they found numerous packets of cash, wrapped in tin foil, slotted in between mattresses. The widow had lived through the Great Depression, had seen a run on banks, and decided she would never face that kind of risk again.

The ruler in Jesus' parable is an investor. He calls ten servants, gives each one the equivalent of three months wages, and tells them to "put it to work." Any level of risk is met by the returning master with *massive* reward—a chance to rule over cities. The master gives graciously and rewards even more graciously for all…all, that is, except the guy who wrapped seed money up, not in tin foil, but in a napkin. That guy opted out. He did not trust the master's character and he wanted nothing to do with the master's economy. Just so you know: the master was not pleased.

Some who read this parable will struggle with the master's harshness, but the real issue for me is all wrapped up in that napkin. Jesus, our Master, recklessly invests his grace in us, all but begging us to place our trust in Him, to do something, anything. He wills us to gamble because no matter what happens to our investments, we are safe.

Jesus, thank you for enlisting us in your economy of grace.

ENLIVEN OUR STONY HEARTS
(LUKE 19:28-40)

> [37] *When he came near the place where the road goes down the Mount of Olives, the whole crowd of disciples began joyfully to praise God in loud voices for all the miracles they had seen:* [38] *"Blessed is the king who comes in the name of the Lord!" "Peace in heaven and glory in the highest!"* [39] *Some of the Pharisees in the crowd said to Jesus, "Teacher, rebuke your disciples!"* [40] *"I tell you," he replied, "if they keep quiet, the stones will cry out."*

When I attended my first Dallas Stars hockey game, I was not prepared for how this unfamiliar sport would lure me in. When our team scored its first goal, I observed myself rising rapidly from my seat, almost involuntarily, and shouting out my praise for our team (I remember it well, because I inadvertently knocked my Dr. Pepper out of the cup holder in the process).

Praise is fitting. When glory passes by, as when Jesus rides upon that portable throne of a colt, how could fragments of psalms and shouts of praise not rise from within? Still, the religious professionals watching nearby deemed the whole display offensive. They instructed Jesus to stifle the praise of his reckless disciples. But if they quieted, Jesus said, "the stones will cry out." His glory will be acknowledged, one way or another, even if our stony hearts remain quiet.

> *"When morning gilds the skies, our hearts awaking cry: May Jesus Christ be praised!"*[6]

CLEANING HOUSE
(LUKE 19:41-48)

[41] As he approached Jerusalem and saw the city, he wept over it [42] and said, "If you, even you, had only known on this day what would bring you peace—but now it is hidden from your eyes. [43] The days will come upon you when your enemies will build an embankment against you and encircle you and hem you in on every side. [44] They will dash you to the ground, you and the children within your walls. They will not leave one stone on another, because you did not recognize the time of God's coming to you."

This is one of the most poignant scenes in this gospel. Before entering the magnificent Temple complex—the spiritual heart of the city—Jesus weeps. Does he do so because he knows the Temple's fate? Does Jesus weep because Roman soldiers will gut this architectural marvel, leaving its few remaining stones a "wailing wall"? Or does Jesus mourn over its present spiritual rot, knowing that the Temple's ultimate demise will be triggered from within? For the moment, Jesus directs his prophetic anger toward those who subvert the rightful place of worship and prayer in God's *house*.

We often speak of spaces in our church building as being "multi-purpose"—the same lobby where worshippers greet one another on a Sunday morning can host supper tables on a Sunday night. Sadly, a worshiper's heart is multi-purpose, too. We often enter holy spaces distracted by unholy desires. We are so self-absorbed that we are unprepared for the time of Christ's visitation (v. 44). I fear how often the Lord weeps over our ignorance, misunderstanding, greed, and resistance to His countercultural teaching.

Jesus, continue to clean house, as painful as such cleaning must be.

AUDITING JESUS' CREDENTIALS
(LUKE 20:1-8)

> *¹ One day as Jesus was teaching the people in the temple courts and proclaiming the good news, the chief priests and the teachers of the law, together with the elders, came up to him. ² "Tell us by what authority you are doing these things," they said. "Who gave you this authority?" ³ He replied, "I will also ask you a question. Tell me: ⁴ John's baptism—was it from heaven, or of human origin?"*

One of the key serving positions for members in our church is "deacon." We have a process for assessing deacon candidates and presenting them to our church for a vote. While that vote is where their "formal" authority comes from, the way they tend to get nominated is that many people see that person "deaconing" (not a real word) "without a license" (not a real crime) over a significant period. It is as if the prior presence of Christ in their lives authorizes them to serve before the church ever gets around to formalizing it.

As Luke 20 opens, those most obsessed with formal religious authority interrupt Jesus' proclamation of the gospel to ask him to flash his credentials. Jesus responds with a momentum-stopping question about the undeniably powerful ministry of the (uncredentialed) John the

Baptist. The religious leaders caucus, vacillate between their own desire for control and fear of the people who revere John, and compose a political answer to Jesus' theological question: "We don't know…" I guess it turns out the authority of the gospel is self-authenticating, much to the chagrin of its opponents.

Jesus, your gospel does not need my vote.

THE THRILL OF DEFEAT
(LUKE 20:9-18)

¹⁷ Jesus looked directly at them and asked, "Then what is the meaning of that which is written: 'The stone the builders rejected has become the cornerstone'? ¹⁸ Everyone who falls on that stone will be broken to pieces; anyone on whom it falls will be crushed."

I once heard a fiction writer state that a story's power often comes in the reversal of a pattern. The big bad wolf so easily blows down the straw and wood houses of the first two little pigs, she said, that we are surprised when the brick house stands firm and the big bad wolf ends up in the pot of soup at the bottom of the chimney!

In Jesus' parable, I expect the reversal to come earlier. Arrogant and violent tenants seize a vineyard that a distant owner planted and begin to fancy themselves as owners. A pattern is formed—three of the owner's men are sent to collect a portion of the harvest, and each one is treated worse than the one before. When the owner decides to send, not one of his employees but rather "my son, whom I love," I could see a literary scenario where the son reigns down all the righteous fury of the father. But this beloved son is not only cast out of the vineyard that belongs to his father, but he is also beaten like the others—and then he is killed.

Yes, eventually the pattern is reversed, as the owner exacts vengeance on the evil tenants (v. 16), but for me, the plot turns on the son's defeat. This ultimate rejection, the murder of the son, is a beginning, his cast-out corpse the new foundation of mercy upon which our new vineyard is constructed (v. 17). This is the climax, the unlikely triumph of defeat.

Jesus, your rejection has become
our foundation.

WHEN JESUS BLOWS OUR COVER
(LUKE 20:20-26)

> [22] *"Is it right for us to pay taxes to Caesar or not?"* [23] *He saw through their duplicity and said to them,* [24] *"Show me a denarius. Whose image and inscription are on it?" "Caesar's,"* *they replied.* [25] *He said to them, "Then give back to Caesar what is Caesar's, and to God what is God's."*

In a graduate seminar I listened as my brilliant theology professor, a skilled debater, recounted this story: two young, well-dressed missionaries on bicycles knocked on his door one day and asked to come inside. "Yes, please," was his enthusiastic response. Hearing that they attempted to enter into a theological debate with him, I actually felt sorry for those boys.

This came to mind as I pictured the "spies" of verse 20, first eavesdropping on Jesus, then feigning sincerity in front of him and flattering him (v. 21), hoping to trick him into saying something that would provide the basis of his arrest. Their binary question—"Is it right for us to pay taxes to Caesar or not?"—invites Jesus to wade into the murky waters of church-state relations (with the name of "Caesar" rolled into the equation like a hand grenade).

Jesus' masterful answer refuses to rule out the responsibilities of being a good citizen, but even more so calls upon his questioners to "give back" to "God what is God's" (v. 25). There the spies stand, their covers blown before God's Son, silenced by his answer (v. 26), left to ponder all many ways they (and *we*) owe God a debt we cannot afford.

Jesus, only your mercy can silence
our inner debates.

THE LORD OF THE LIVING
(LUKE 20:27-40)

37 "But in the account of the burning bush, even Moses showed that the dead rise, for he calls the Lord 'the God of Abraham, and the God of Isaac, and the God of Jacob.' 38 He is not the God of the dead, but of the living, for to him all are alive."

If Jerusalem had a Polo Club back in the day, the Sadducees would have run it. They were members of the aristocracy and were known for, among other things, their refusal to believe in unsophisticated doctrines like the resurrection from the dead. Accordingly, they attempted to set Jesus up by sharing a hypothetical with a ridiculous premise (a poor woman who has been widowed seven times to seven brothers) to show how foolish the concept of a future heaven must be. 'Just imagine that poor widow trying to figure out which heavenly husband she belongs to!' For this and many other reasons, they concluded heaven must be a fairy tale.

Jesus responded with theological nuance, addressing the nature both of earthly marriage as well the mysteries of eternal life in heaven (vv. 34-36). But what catches my attention is Jesus' reference in verse 37 to the "burning bush." Back in Exodus 3, Moses stood barefoot before this curiously burning shrub, and heard God speak from the bush, identifying Himself as "the God of Abraham, the God of Isaac, and the God of Jacob." He was, and is, the God of dead patriarchs who still live. How much more will our Resurrected Christ fill us with eternal life and love?

> "Earth's crammed with heaven,
> And every common bush afire with God,
> But only he who sees takes off his shoes;
> The rest sit round and pluck blackberries."
> (Elizabeth Barrett Browning)

SEEING OVER THE SLANT
(LUKE 20:41-21:4)

⁴⁵ While all the people were listening, Jesus said to his disciples, ⁴⁶ "Beware of the teachers of the law. They like to walk around in flowing robes and love to be greeted with respect in the marketplaces and have the most important seats in the synagogues and the places of honor at banquets. ⁴⁷ They devour widows' houses and for a show make lengthy prayers. These men will be punished most severely."

In the amusement parks of the early twentieth century, proprietors were fond of building what they called a "Tilthouse." These windowless shacks, with dark and winding entrances, were built on an angle. Once inside, with no outside frame of reference, participants saw "strange phenomena" like water defying the laws of gravity by rolling uphill. I actually went inside something like it during my childhood; I marveled at the phenomena even as I had to hold onto the guardrails to keep from tumbling over.

In today's passage, Jesus exposes that what passes for normal in the religious life of the nation is slanted. It is slanted to view Jesus as David's lesser relative when Jesus was in fact David's "Lord" (v. 41-44). It is slanted to view the "teachers of the law" as paragons of virtue when their love for God pales in comparison to their love for self and pomp and ill-gotten offerings (45-47). It is slanted to judge the value of people's contributions by the mere dollar signs, when poor widows truly reveal the essence of generosity (21:1-4).

Sometimes what we need most is for Jesus to open the windows—to let us see our distorted piety and our Savior's eye for hidden generosity (21:2).

Jesus, expose the sinful slant in our religion.

NOT 'WHEN' OR 'WHAT' BUT 'HOW' (LUKE 21:5-28)

> [5] *Some of his disciples were remarking about how the temple was adorned with beautiful stones and with gifts dedicated to God. But Jesus said,* [6] *"As for what you see here, the time will come when not one stone will be left on another; every one of them will be thrown down."* [7] *"Teacher," they asked, "when will these things happen? And what will be the sign that they are about to take place?"* [8] *He replied: "Watch out that you are not deceived. For many will come in my name, claiming, 'I am he,' and, 'The time is near.' Do not follow them."*

Maybe it is just me, but does it seem like Jesus tends to answer very different questions than the ones the disciples ask? After Jesus warns his disciples that this Temple is not nearly as sturdy as they assume (vv. 5-6), his disciples want to know the "when" and the "what." When will the scary stuff happen? What signs can prepare us to know when we are on the verge of the scary?

When it comes to signs, Jesus talks more about false signs than authentic ones (vv. 8-9). At times it is hard to know whether Jesus is preparing the disciples for a near-term cataclysm (the destruction of Jerusalem and the Temple) or the ultimate world cataclysm that pre-cedes "the Son of Man coming in a cloud with power and great glory" (vv. 25-27).

We naturally want the insider-trading scoop on the "when" and "what" of world-shaking events, but Jesus is much more concerned with preparing us for the "how" of surviving the worst life can throw at us. He wants to build a deep endurance in us, to give us the faith to trust that he will supply us with what we need the most (v. 15)—the grace that causes us to lift our heads when everything else is falling down (v. 28).

Jesus, you lift our heads to see that our
"redemption is drawing near."

READING THE LEAVES
(LUKE 21:29-38)

29 He told them this parable: "Look at the fig tree and all the trees. 30 When they sprout leaves, you can see for yourselves and know that summer is near. 31 Even so, when you see these things happening, you know that the kingdom of God is near."

My college Greek professor would assign us whole chapters of the New Testament to translate, and then in class he would start with the front row and work his way to the back, having each student read their translation of a consecutive verse. One day, completely unprepared, I calculated how many students were in front of me, and then translated a single verse. When it came time for the professor to call on me to recite my translation, my ruse worked like a charm! I couldn't help bragging to a seat mate about my good fortune (and deception!) as we were walking down the hall after class. Suddenly, I heard the booming voice of my professor (who apparently had been walking a few feet behind us): "Did you learn much Greek that way?"

That painful memory colors my reading of this passage. Too many Christians, past and present, seem to prefer calculating a moment for Christ's return over living in a daily state of readiness. My reading of Chapter 21 is that while Jesus is not keen on the idea of our trying to pinpoint his return, neither does he want us to put his return out of our minds altogether. As his parable of the fig tree suggests (vv. 29-31), just as spring leaves point to the changing of the season, so will Christ's world-altering resurrection signal a new season for the world. And Jesus wants us to "read the leaves," as it were, and to live "ready." What some may view as terrifying is better seen as hopeful: of all the things in our lives that are vulnerable to sudden disaster, Christ's word of promise can always be counted on.

> *"So don't be afraid, little flock. For it gives your Father great happiness to give you the Kingdom" (Luke 12:32 NLT).*

THE COMING COLLISION
(LUKE 22:1-6)

¹ Now the Festival of Unleavened Bread, called the Passover, was approaching, ² and the chief priests and the teachers of the law were looking for some way to get rid of Jesus, for they were afraid of the people. ³ Then Satan entered Judas, called Iscariot, one of the Twelve. ⁴ And Judas went to the chief priests and the officers of the temple guard and discussed with them how he might betray Jesus.

In Thomas Hardy's 1912 poem, "The Convergence of the Twain (Lines on the loss of the *Titanic*)," the poet meditates upon the *converging* of that "smart ship" with the hidden iceberg. Two entities which seemed to be so remote from one another became "twin halves of one august event."

In the death of Jesus, multiple events converge. The first, the Passover, places Jesus in the middle of the holy Jewish calendar (indeed, it places Jesus on the menu as the Passover Lamb). Simultaneously, Satan (v. 3) conspires to put Jesus in the crosshairs of an evil plot via human accomplices. The "chief priests" and Temple officers are the central conspirators, the "money men" who fund the project. Judas is the inside man, positioned by proximity to deliver a surprise betrayal of Jesus.

Of the wreck of the *Titanic*, Hardy says, "No mortal eye could see/The intimate welding of their later history." The same was true for the mortal eyes of the disciples preparing the Passover meal. The eyes of Jesus, however, saw it all, and still refused to turn the ship around.

Jesus, out of love for us you refused to thwart your own betrayal.

BLESSEDLY TRAPPED
IN A MOMENT
(LUKE 22:7-23)

> [17] *After taking the cup, he gave thanks and said, "Take this and divide it among you.* [18] *For I tell you I will not drink again from the fruit of the vine until the kingdom of God comes." * [19] *And he took bread, gave thanks and broke it, and gave it to them, saying, "This is my body given for you; do this in remembrance of me." * [20] *In the same way, after the supper he took the cup, saying, "This cup is the new covenant in my blood, which is poured out for you."*

The 'day' comes first, a day of Passover preparation (v. 7). Everything goes smoothly, as the disciples are mysteriously guided to a large and well-furnished room to prepare the meal. Next comes the 'hour' (v. 14)—a time for a Passover meal that, for some reason, Jesus has "eagerly desired" to share with his disciples. Luke mentions two cups here (vv. 17, 20), and scholars are not in complete agreement about how Jesus manages both to observe the traditional Passover celebration and somehow remake it. What does become clear, however, as the *day* of Passover leads into the *hour* of the meal, is that Jesus wants his disciples riveted to this *moment*—a moment of extreme generosity, as Jesus freely gives the bread and the cup and, by extension, his life.

Two thousand years later, Christians have not been able to move beyond that moment; Jesus has asked us to remain within it—"do this in remembrance of me" (v. 19). We still sit around His table, so distracted and frightened and confused (v. 23), needing Jesus to call us to attention. We still worry that our hands are those which betray the one who feeds us the bread of life (v. 22). We still long for the fullest experience of His Kingdom. We still grieve, and we still marvel that His broken body and shed blood have somehow made us whole.

Jesus, keep us in the moment.

THE GREATEST
(LUKE 22:24-30)

²⁴ A dispute also arose among them as to which of them was considered to be greatest. ²⁵ Jesus said to them, "The kings of the Gentiles lord it over them; and those who exercise authority over them call themselves Benefactors. ²⁶ But you are not to be like that. Instead, the greatest among you should be like the youngest, and the one who rules like the one who serves. ²⁷ For who is greater, the one who is at the table or the one who serves? Is it not the one who is at the table? But I am among you as one who serves."

In 1964, when Cassius Clay (later Muhammad Ali) stepped into the ring to fight Sonny Liston, the reigning opinion of boxing punditry was that Liston would quickly dispatch the upstart. When the reverse happened, Clay shouted into the microphone of Howard Cosell: "I am the greatest! I am the king of the world!" Were life defined in terms of the late 20th century boxing ring, he would have been correct.

If you expand the ring to the ends of the earth, the contest looks different. Yes, the powerful still seek titles, and they do so by humiliating all pretenders to their thrones (v. 25). But Jesus redefined greatness. He made it something to be searched for among the quiet obscurity of dirty pots and pans being scrubbed in a room far from the banquet hall. Jesus' greatness humiliates those of us who believe we are great, who are prone to subtract stars off Yelp reviews because "the service was lacking." Jesus, the epitome of greatness, even now, reigns among us "as one who serves" (v. 27).

Jesus, you embody greatness by serving us.

TRUTH IN A TIME CAPSULE
(LUKE 22:31-38)

[31] *"Simon, Simon, Satan has asked to sift all of you as wheat. [32] But I have prayed for you, Simon, that your faith may not fail. And when you have turned back, strengthen your brothers." [33] But he replied, "Lord, I am ready to go with you to prison and to death." [34] Jesus answered, "I tell you, Peter, before the rooster crows today, you will deny three times that you know me."*

In one of modern cinema's greatest tearjerker scenes, the dying mom Emma (Debra Winger) in *Terms of Endearment* has her last conversation with her two young sons. Emma and Tommy (the older one) have been in a rough patch for some time, and he is obviously struggling to share his deepest emotions with her. Emma predicts that one day Tommy will regret his reticence. "And maybe you're gonna feel badly, because you never told me. But don't—I know that you love me. So don't ever do that to yourself, all right?"

Jesus, having entered his last hours on earth before the cross, puts bracing and hopeful words into a time capsule for his unprepared disciples. He warns an overconfident Peter that his soul will become a battlefield between Satanic intimidation and divine intercession.

Ultimately, Jesus assures him that his own prayers will win the battle for Peter's soul, and that Peter should later pay the grace forward: "strengthen your brothers" (vv. 31-32).

Jesus often has more to say to us than we can comprehend in the moment. On that terrifying night, his disciples misunderstood (v. 38). Still, they had Jesus' words and Jesus' prayers and even his promises that "return" from the tailspin of sin was possible (v. 32). These precious gifts that would remain, long after Jesus Himself was gone from this earth.

Jesus, your grace is given to us before we even need it.

THE BOTTOM OF THE
STAIRCASE
(LUKE 22:39-46)

⁴² "Father, if you are willing, take this cup from me; yet not my will, but yours be done." ⁴³ An angel from heaven appeared to him and strengthened him. ⁴⁴ And being in anguish, he prayed more earnestly, and his sweat was like drops of blood falling to the ground.

Some commentators say it is most helpful to read Luke's version of the Gethsemane prayer retreat as if the passage descends and then ascends a short staircase (scholars call it a "chiasm").

On the top step, Jesus teaches. Twice, he urges his disciples to pray for God's help in avoiding the terrible temptations which lurk in this dark time (vv. 40, 46).

On the next step down, Jesus prays. He initiates his prayer by kneeling (v. 41) and later concludes it by rising (v. 45).

On the third step down, Jesus wrestles. He is clearly wrestling in prayer with this "cup" of judgment that he intuits God is leading him to drink (v. 42), and this wrestling is physically as well as spiritually agonizing (v. 44).

The most important step in any chiasm, the one that highlights the central theme, is the bottom step. Here, Jesus is strengthened. In verse 43, an angel *strengthened*

Jesus to drink the dreaded cup and prepare for the ultimate battle of the cross.

None of us will ever know what strength it took for Jesus to descend to drink the dregs of our judgment and then walk back up to face what would come next. And it feels almost trivial to compare my current dark times with Jesus sweating drops of blood in Gethsemane. Still, I pray that for you and for me, when we are at the very bottom of life, we will know that we are not alone. The same Jesus who teaches us to pray also prays for us, wrestles evil on our behalf, and provides unexpected strength in our lowest moments.

Jesus, you are our strength
at the bottom of life.

WHAT ADVERSITY REVEALED
(LUKE 22:47-53)

50 And one of them struck the servant of the high priest, cutting off his right ear. 51 But Jesus answered, "No more of this!" And he touched the man's ear and healed him. 52 Then Jesus said to the chief priests, the officers of the temple guard, and the elders, who had come for him, "Am I leading a rebellion, that you have come with swords and clubs? 53 Every day I was with you in the temple courts, and you did not lay a hand on me. But this is your hour— when darkness reigns."

I first heard the maxim—*"Adversity does not build character; it reveals it"*—from an empathic friend during a troubling season in ministry. He meant it as a word of affirmation, but I received it more as an X-ray of my barely concealed character deficiencies.

In the crucible of extreme adversity in Luke 22, Jesus' holy character shines out in the approaching gloom. So much of the gospel story is compressed into this chaotic scene. Jesus' opponents are conspiring against him, his disciple is betraying him, his other disciples are misreading him (vv. 49-51), and seemingly everyone misunderstands his mission (v. 52). As at the beginning of his public ministry, during his 40 days' fast in the wilderness, Jesus again faces off against the forces of darkness (v. 53).

But he does not allow the chaos to move him off course. Still he teaches (v. 47, 53), and his words pierce like a sword (v. 48). Still he reaches out his hand to heal the wounds that Evil recklessly dishes out. Still he submits to the awful plan God has laid out for him, the unrelenting path to secure our redemption—becoming, in his crucified body, that place where justice and mercy kiss.

"Love and faithfulness meet together;
righteousness and peace kiss each other."
(Psalm 85:10)

WHAT THE FACE TRIES
TO CONCEAL
(LUKE 22:54-62)

⁵⁹ About an hour later another asserted, "Certainly this fellow was with him, for he is a Galilean." ⁶⁰ Peter replied, "Man, I don't know what you're talking about!" Just as he was speaking, the rooster crowed. ⁶¹ The Lord turned and looked straight at Peter. Then Peter remembered the word the Lord had spoken to him: "Before the rooster crows today, you will disown me three times." ⁶² And he went outside and wept bitterly.

Whenever my mom feared I was misleading her about something, she would say, "Look at me." Sometimes, she would reach for my ears and pull my face down toward her upturned, investigating eyes. She believed she could read the truth my words concealed, and she was usually right.

In the firelight of that awful night, as Peter followed the newly arrested Jesus "at a distance," his face is more open to scrutiny than he realizes. In the firelight, a servant girl "looks closely" at Peter's anguished face and concludes that he was with Jesus. Others agree, especially noting their shared Galilean idiosyncrasies (v. 59).

Three times, Peter's false words attempt to paper over the truth.

When the rooster sounded the alarm, Peter could not conceal his face from Jesus—"The Lord turned and looked straight at Peter" (v. 61). Across the chasm that separated the disciple from his master, Peter's face can be seen with unflinching clarity. No longer attempting the charade, Peter exits the campfire crowd and weeps "bitterly." Thankfully, this won't be the last time Jesus peers into Peter's eyes.

Jesus, you see straight through us.

PROPHET, PRIEST, AND KING
(LUKE 22:63-71)

> [67] *"If you are the Messiah," they said, "tell us." Jesus answered, "If I tell you, you will not believe me,* [68] *and if I asked you, you would not answer.* [69] *But from now on, the Son of Man will be seated at the right hand of the mighty God."*

Theologians often use a trio of roles to describe the work of Christ on our behalf. Combining and fulfilling the major roles of spiritual leadership in the Hebrew Scriptures, Jesus is our *prophet, priest,* and *king.* Like a prophet, he proclaims the truth of God to us; like a priest, he facilitates our forgiveness with God through the sacrifice of his own life; like a king, he governs and overcomes the world.

We're left to assume that Jesus' accusers could not see these roles. The guards who cruelly blindfolded and beat him and begged him to "prophesy" (v. 65)? They did not know this prophet knew the deepest truths about each of them. The religious leaders who "led" Jesus before them like a lamb offered up for a priestly sacrifice (v. 66)? How could they have known God would use their cruelty as a stage to enact his mercy?

The hardest truths for Jesus' accusers to swallow was that the prisoner before them would one day be vindicated as the King of Kings, "seated at the right hand of the mighty God" (v. 69). Astonishingly, Jesus feels no need to debate these truths. He *is* the prophet who tells us about God, the priest who reconciles us with God, and the king who leads us into the Kingdom of God.

> *"Jesus, Savior, reigneth forever and ever!*
> *Crown him, crown him! Prophet, and priest,*
> *and king!" (Fanny Crosby)*

'THE LORD HAS TAKEN AWAY'

(LUKE 23:1-24:53)

Job, the legendary sufferer of the Old Testament, famously said amid the rubble of his old and comfortable life, "The Lord gave and the Lord has taken away; may the name of the Lord be praised" (Job 1:21). Yet the level of Job's suffering only anticipates what Jesus will endure in the pages ahead of us. In choosing to place the punishment of humanity's sins on Jesus, the Lord will take away everything any of us might have chosen to rely upon—Jesus' reputation, his friends, his legal rights, his dignity, his clothes, his blood, his breath.

Somehow, in the ensuing centuries, Christians have looked upon this scene of Jesus' passion and inverted the words of Job. Through Christ, we have learned to say, "The Lord has taken away *our sin*, and the Lord *gave grace, resurrection, vision, the bread, the cup, and hope*; may the name of the Lord Jesus be praised."

WHEN PEOPLE SHOW US
WHO THEY ARE
(LUKE 23:1-7)

² And they began to accuse him, saying, "We have found this man subverting our nation. He opposes payment of taxes to Caesar and claims to be Messiah, a king."³ So Pilate asked Jesus, "Are you the king of the Jews?" "You have said so," Jesus replied.⁴ Then Pilate announced to the chief priests and the crowd, "I find no basis for a charge against this man."

Whenever I'm hiring someone, I try to reflect on a quote attributed to Maya Angelou: "When people show you who they are, believe them." In other words, if an applicant arrives late for an interview, or responds in a passive-aggressive manner to your challenging questions, this is likely not an anomaly. They are showing you who they are.

In today's passage, the participants unveil their true identities. The religious leaders continue to disappoint, displaying an eagerness to distort and even lie about what Jesus has said and done (v. 2). When they are initially rebuffed, they double-down on their verbal aggression (v. 5). Pilate also lets slip what will soon become painfully clear: he is a man at war with himself. Pilate vacillates between the convictions of his conscience ("I find no basis for a charge against this man") and the expediencies of his predicament (*let's ship him off to Herod!*).

Jesus, too, continues to show us who he is. His quiet courage before Pilate speaks loudly. While Jesus is not the political subversive that the religious leaders claim him to be, he is nevertheless 'stirring up' the people. And he will continue to do so.

Jesus, you turn our world upside down
(Acts 17:6).

JESUS, CORNERED
(LUKE 23:8-12)

[8] When Herod saw Jesus, he was greatly pleased, because for a long time he had been wanting to see him. From what he had heard about him, he hoped to see him perform a sign of some sort. [9] He plied him with many questions, but Jesus gave him no answer. [10] The chief priests and the teachers of the law were standing there, vehemently accusing him. [11] Then Herod and his soldiers ridiculed and mocked him. Dressing him in an elegant robe, they sent him back to Pilate.

I picture Jesus cornered, unarmed, with a mixed mob of 'church and state' circling him.

On the 'state' side, Herod initially plays the 'good cop'. *Jesus, I have been so wanting to meet you. I hope you don't mind but I have a million questions. Where should I begin? And oh, by the way, I would be so pleased if you'd be willing to perform one of those supernatural tricks you have been known to do.* When Herod is unable to co-opt Jesus, he resorts to the 'bad cop' mode that better suits his character, complete with bullying and sinister comedy. All the while, the 'church' side sings backup with a continual refrain of accusation (v. 10). Ultimately, Herod and his soldiers drape Jesus in an elegant robe, and there he stands alone, the ironic king.

How do you respond when cornered? Charge forward with arms flailing? Zig and zag and try to run away? Say anything, literally anything, to secure an unlikely escape? King Jesus, opposed by the combined powers of church and state, facing a war of words and worse, chooses silent restraint as his only response.

Jesus, your silence speaks profoundly to us.

REASON V. RAGE
(LUKE 23:13-25)

²² For the third time he spoke to them: "Why? What crime has this man committed? I have found in him no grounds for the death penalty. Therefore I will have him punished and then release him." ²³ But with loud shouts they insistently demanded that he be crucified, and their shouts prevailed. ²⁴ So Pilate decided to grant their demand.

Here is a battle between cold logic and hot rage. Pilate, like a defense attorney giving a summation, lines up his reasons to release Jesus. The claim that Jesus was inciting a "rebellion" (v. 14) was not substantiated. Two different rulers (Herod and Pilate himself) have found no basis to convict him. Pilate cannot conceive of any crime Jesus may have committed which would warrant the "death penalty." On three different occasions, Pilate coolly argues the logic of his case to release Jesus.

Rage, rising in the cries of the crowd, surges forward like a forest fire. The mob does not engage Pilate; they shout him down. They seek the release of a murderer named Barabbas instead of the Jesus with whom Pilate finds no fault. Their "loud shouts" and insistent "demands" for crucifixion ultimately "prevail." When Pilate caves (v. 24), rage wins (v. 25). Pilate released

Barabbas (whose name means "son of the father"), and surrendered over Jesus, the sinless Son of the Heavenly Father.

Later, when Luke's story continues in the book of Acts, we will discover that logic and emotion need not be enemies. Indeed, one 20th century preacher (David Martyn Lloyd-Jones) has defined the kind of gospel preaching the Holy Spirit launches in Acts 2 as "logic on fire." All that lies on the other side of the resurrection. For now, madness reigns.

Jesus, your Father delights in your costly obedience (Luke 9:35).

THE SCENE OF THE COLLISION
(LUKE 23:26-31)

> *26 As the soldiers led him away, they seized Simon from Cyrene, who was on his way in from the country, and put the cross on him and made him carry it behind Jesus. 27 A large number of people followed him, including women who mourned and wailed for him.*

Simon of Cyrene got T-Boned (at least, that's my best reconstruction of what happened). Simon, a Passover pilgrim traveling from North Africa, finds himself the victim of an unexpected collision with the Jesus-Death-Train. Simon will walk away from this encounter, but not until he temporarily absorbs a relatively small portion of the burden Jesus carries toward Calvary. He likely carries the horizontal crossbeam all the way to vertical post at the place of Jesus' crucifixion. Weeping women also trail behind the wreckage of Jesus and his cross, and Jesus warns them that the forces of evil that fall now upon him will one day engulf their whole people (vv. 29-31).

What will happen to those who are blessed to walk away from this collision? Do their tears and wailing (v. 27) turn to shouts of joy three days later? Are they forever chastened by the enormous irrationality of evil, and forever astonished by the love that keeps walking, one agonizing step after another, toward the cross? And what about those of us who have watched Jesus carry our worst failures on his shoulders? Are we forever "scarred" by the sudden impact of grace?

Jesus, you carried our burden all the way to the end.

FLIPPING THE SCRIPT
(LUKE 23:32-43)

> [32] *Two other men, both criminals, were also led out with him to be executed.* [33] *When they came to the place called the Skull, they crucified him there, along with the criminals—one on his right, the other on his left.* [34] *Jesus said, "Father, forgive them, for they do not know what they are doing." And they divided up his clothes by casting lots.* [35] *The people stood watching, and the rulers even sneered at him. They said, "He saved others; let him save himself if he is God's Messiah, the Chosen One."*

When I'm studying a Bible passage, I sometimes pretend that I discovered it as a fragment of paper, like a crumpled-up flyer nesting against a curb. I try to imagine I know nothing about the fragment's origin as I unfold the wrinkled page and read it on its own terms. This fragment pulls my mind in opposing directions. After all, we know how we are supposed to feel when criminals are paraded to the place of their final judgment. Even if we politely refrain from righteous taunts, even if we disagree with the manner of punishment, we believe in justice. We believe criminals deserve to be punished.

But what of the criminal in the middle (v. 33)? He doesn't fit the script. He disturbs us. Naked, he prays grace over those who steal his only possessions (v. 34). Powerless, he promises a penitent man a place in His kingdom. Even amidst the sneers and taunts tossed at him, we cannot dodge words like "saved" (four times!) and "Messiah" and "Chosen One" and, yes, "king." In our reading of this fragment, something flips. The criminal in the middle turns our taunts into pleas for mercy.

Jesus, Savior, Messiah, Chosen One, Crucified King, remember us too (v. 42).

WHEN MOCKERY MELTS
IN OUR MOUTHS
(LUKE 23:44-49)

⁴⁶ Jesus called out with a loud voice, "Father, into your hands I commit my spirit." When he had said this, he breathed his last. ⁴⁷ The centurion, seeing what had happened, praised God and said, "Surely this was a righteous man." ⁴⁸ When all the people who had gathered to witness this sight saw what took place, they beat their breasts and went away.

Do you know that moment in a horror movie when the cocky, naughty teenagers realize they're in trouble? When life grows suddenly dark, and they are alone, and something much more powerful than them is lurking? I almost feel that way when I read this passage. The power the onlookers confront, however, is righteous rather than sinister. Still, it is terrifying.

Place yourself in the sandals of those who observed the crucifixion. Feel what they feel as literal darkness falls in the early afternoon (v. 44), as the Temple curtain is rent by invisible hands (v. 45). Listen to them overhearing Jesus' last, loud breaths which proclaim an undiluted faith (v. 46). Watch them hear a centurion reverse course on Jesus' innocence (v. 47). Whatever bravado these onlookers brought to this crucifixion has now vanished. Those who came to see the "sight" (think *circus*) now return home shamed and visibly shaken with grief (v. 48).

There are worse things than the terror that overtakes us when we gaze upon holy love. Jesus endured them when he "descended to the lower, earthly regions" (Ephesians 4:9).

Jesus, your righteousness shines through the spectacle of the cross.

PREPARING FOR OPENING DAY
(LUKE 23:50-56)

> *50 Now there was a man named Joseph, a member of the Council, a good and upright man, 51 who had not consented to their decision and action. He came from the Judean town of Arimathea, and he himself was waiting for the kingdom of God. 52 Going to Pilate, he asked for Jesus' body. 53 Then he took it down, wrapped it in linen cloth and placed it in a tomb cut in the rock, one in which no one had yet been laid.*

In a rather dark section of a stark New Testament letter, Jude warns of divisive people who "follow natural instincts" and, not surprisingly, "do not have the Spirit" (v. 19). You could say that the entire 23rd chapter of Luke has been dominated by the sinful instincts of people who conspire to murder God's Son.

Towards the end of the chapter, we find women and a man whose instincts rise from a different source. Joseph of Arimathea, while a member of the religious body which advocated for Jesus' death, was a "good and upright man" who disagreed with their decision. His heart was tuned to the coming of "the kingdom of God" (vv. 50-51). Joseph leverages his own privilege to secure and care for the body of Jesus (v. 52-53), and to provide a pristine tomb. Similarly, some women disciples who had been following Jesus since Galilee traced the movements of his corpse and gathered funeral supplies for his body.

Joseph and these women could not have conceived the roles they were playing in God's grand performance—Joseph, building a theatre for Jesus' resurrection, and these women, purchasing the first tickets for the show.

Jesus, you provide the holy instincts which
lead us back to you.

GUMSHOE ANGELS
(LUKE 24:1-12)

⁴ While they were wondering about this, suddenly two men in clothes that gleamed like lightning stood beside them. ⁵ In their fright the women bowed down with their faces to the ground, but the men said to them, "Why do you look for the living among the dead? ⁶ He is not here; he has risen! Remember how he told you, while he was still with you in Galilee: ⁷ 'The Son of Man must be delivered over to the hands of sinners, be crucified and on the third day be raised again.'"

It sets up like the climax of a classic mystery novel. After establishing the vital clues of *when* (early Sunday morning) and *who* (mourning women) and *where* (the newly exposed tomb), we are confronted with the mystifying *how* and *why* of the missing "body of the Lord Jesus" (v. 3). That's when a pair of gleaming 'detectives' step forward. Reminding the women of all the clues they have missed (vv. 6-7), these angels present the solution to the mystery: *He has risen!*

On further reflection, the angels do not so much solve the mystery as *unveil* it. When the women relate their discovery to the eleven disciples, their words sound less like a mystery solved than a fantasy spun (v. 11).

Still, there was enough credible evidence to lure Peter to the empty tomb and prompt some detective work of his own (v. 12). Ever since, millions have followed Peter's path into that beautiful mystery, into that glorious absence: "He is not here…"

> *Jesus, your glorious resurrection is the mystery*
> *that sustains us.*

THE BREAD THAT MAKES
THE SANDWICH
(LUKE 24:13-27)

¹⁵ As they talked and discussed these things with each other, Jesus himself came up and walked along with them; ¹⁶ but they were kept from recognizing him. ¹⁷ He asked them, "What are you discussing together as you walk along?" They stood still, their faces downcast. ¹⁸ One of them, named Cleopas, asked him, "Are you the only one visiting Jerusalem who does not know the things that have happened there in these days?"

Think of our passage as a sandwich. The bread is Jesus, who asks a question in verse 17 and later responds to the answers he receives in verse 25. The stuff in the middle, if you will, is where you and I live, where all the truth and doubt and chaos of life is smushed together.

In the muddled middle, with these disciples grappling with "Jesus of Nazareth," I see the making of a classic celebrity profile: Part 1—the dramatic promise of a powerful prophet; Part 2—the tragic fall of the prophet; Part 3—the ongoing rumors and tabloid headlines that the prophet's demise has been drastically overstated. This is life, so we think: sweet *dreams*, dashed *hopes*, and ongoing questions about both.

Perhaps that is why, with this sandwich, our comfort is found in the bread that surrounds us. Whether we recognize him or not, Jesus is always ready to join our conversation (vv. 15-16). And no matter how "slow" we can be to catch on, Jesus is there, patiently directing us back to the Scriptures and to our lives, to his "suffering" and to his "glory," showing himself to be the focal point of everything we hold dear (v. 27).

> *"You hem me in behind and before, and you lay your hand upon me…" (Psalm 139:5)*

THE MOMENT OF CLARITY
(LUKE 24:28-35)

> *29 But they urged him strongly, "Stay with us, for it is nearly evening; the day is almost over." So he went in to stay with them. 30 When he was at the table with them, he took bread, gave thanks, broke it and began to give it to them. 31 Then their eyes were opened and they recognized him, and he disappeared from their sight. 32 They asked each other, "Were not our hearts burning within us while he talked with us on the road and opened the Scriptures to us?"*

The screenwriter Brian Koppelman hosts a podcast called "The Moment." The title reflects Koppelman's goal with each episode. As he interviews writers, musicians, and entrepreneurs, he seeks to discover that "moment" when the light came on and their careers took off.

For the two disciples on the road to Emmaus, we don't have to speculate; Luke tells us clearly. The moment happened after they urged this mysterious stranger they encountered on the road to "stay with us" and brought him home with them. It happened after the sun had set and dinner was hastily placed on the table. It happened after this strange guest was bold to play the role of host, after he gripped the bread in both hands to bless it and distribute it to them.

This was the moment—when eyes were opening (v. 31) and hearts were "burning" (v. 32). When the Bread of Life broke bread with scarred hands, everything suddenly became clear (v. 35).

Jesus, your generosity brings life into clear focus.

THE MERRY PRANKSTER
(LUKE 24:36-43)

> [36] *While they were still talking about this, Jesus himself stood among them and said to them, "Peace be with you."* [37] *They were startled and frightened, thinking they saw a ghost.* [38] *He said to them, "Why are you troubled, and why do doubts rise in your minds?* [39] *Look at my hands and my feet. It is I myself! Touch me and see; a ghost does not have flesh and bones, as you see I have."*

I worked with a guy one time who was a truly committed prankster. He would arrive early to the office and hide down under a coworker's desk. When the crouching colleague heard the office door knob turn, he would suddenly rise up and shout. Mayhem would ensue as the coworker's fright turned to anger and then just as quickly to laughter.

In light of today's passage, would it be irreverent of me to refer to the Resurrected Jesus as a Merry Prankster? When you study his resurrection appearances in the gospel, he does seem to have a habit of suddenly appearing before his disciples and shouting—not "Surprise!"—but "Peace be with you" (v. 36). And judging from their reactions, they cycle through craven fear (v.

37) to troubled doubts (v. 38) to an almost "too good to be true" sense of amazement (v. 41).

I believe Jesus' 'pranks' have a profound purpose. Like electric defibrillator paddles applied to a stopped heart, Jesus shocks the feeble faith of his "startled and frightened" disciples into beating again. He urges them to doubt their doubts while he marshals forth the evidence of scarred hands and feet. He even dines on a meal of broiled fish to prove he is real. Resurrection restores a holy rhythm to our hearts.

Jesus, your risen presence brings us
shocking peace.

YOU SAY GOODBYE,
BUT I SAY HELLO
(LUKE 24:44-53)

49 "I am going to send you what my Father has promised; but stay in the city until you have been clothed with power from on high." 50 When he had led them out to the vicinity of Bethany, he lifted up his hands and blessed them. 51 While he was blessing them, he left them and was taken up into heaven. 52 Then they worshiped him and returned to Jerusalem with great joy.

My dad called them the "Sob Sisters." When, after their honeymoon, my dad had loaded the car to take my mom from her childhood home in New York City to their new home in Texas, her cousins circled around my mom and wailed, prompting my mother to join in. To be fair, the Sob Sisters were only engaging in an extreme form of how we normally react when loved ones leave us.

Curiously, this is not the reaction of the disciples when Jesus ascends to heaven (v. 51). Why is this? Why are not they, of all people, the most desolate at Jesus' departure? Perhaps it is because of the parting gifts Jesus leaves them: minds opened to understand the outrageous promises of the Bible (vv. 45-48), a transcendent mission to preach the possibility of forgiveness *everywhere* (v. 47), and the promised gift which will outfit them "with power from on high" (v. 49)—namely, the Holy Spirit.

Armed with such gifts, promises, and blessings (v. 50), the disciples waving goodbye do not sob but worship with joy, taking the party to the Temple in continual praise. They watch Him ascend, but He never truly leaves them.

Jesus, your blessing on us is eternal.

AFTERWORD

(ACTS 1:11)

"Men of Galilee," they said, "why do you stand here looking into the sky? This same Jesus, who has been taken from you into heaven, will come back in the same way you have seen him go into heaven."

As this little book reaches its conclusion, Luke's literary production continues. His second volume, the Acts of the Apostles, picks up the action approximately where our story ends, as the disciples stand staring at the sky where Jesus has just ascended.

Perhaps this is a helpful resting place for us, as Luke's gospel ends, not so much with a "The End" and rolling credits, but with an angelic reminder to stop staring wistfully into the sky (Acts 1:11) and to prepare for what Jesus has next.

It is good to stare at the sky. It is even better to look a little closer to the ground, at the people around you, and to remember the present love of Jesus for all of us.

ENDNOTES

1. Page 18: Joseph Fitzmyer, Anchor Bible.
2. Page 47: David Garland, *Luke* (Zondervan Exegetical Commentary).
3. Page 163: Wilbur Rees, "Three Dollars Worth of God."
4. Page 164: "Think about what Jesus is actually saying. On the one hand, it is terrifying and unreasonable: in order to gain salvation, life, and reconciliation, you have to lose every amenity, every relationship, every last scrap of the good life you might have. In short, you have to be dead" (Robert Farrar Capon, *Kingdom, Grace, Judgment: Paradox, Outrage, and Vindication in the Parables of Jesus*).
5. Page 175: Robert Farrar Capon, *Kingdom, Grace, Judgment*, 317.
6. Page 196: From an originally German hymn, translated by Edward Caswell.

ABOUT THE AUTHOR

Larry Parsley is the author of two devotionals, including *An Easy Stroll Through a Short Gospel: Meditations on Mark*. In 2023, he became Clinical Professor of Christian Ministry and the Director of Mentoring for Baylor University's Truett Seminary, after serving as senior pastor of Valley Ranch Baptist in Coppell, Texas, for over 23 years. In addition to his connection with Mockingbird Ministries, he also writes for Christianity Today's *Preaching Today* and is a homiletical consultant for SMU's Perkins Center for Preaching Excellence. He is passionate about helping clergy find re-enchantment in their holy callings. Larry and his wife Jaletta have four children and two grand-daughters. He enjoys baseball, Baylor sports, coffee, used bookstores, walking, and dad jokes.

ABOUT MOCKINGBIRD

Founded in 2007, Mockingbird is an organization devoted to connecting the Christian faith with the realities of everyday life in fresh and down-to-earth ways. We do this primarily, but not exclusively, through our publications, conferences, and online resources. To find out more, visit us at mbird.com or e-mail us at info@mbird.com.

Printed in the USA
CPSIA information can be obtained
at www.ICGtesting.com
LVHW090753181123
764187LV00003B/14